INTEGRITY

AT WORK

Ken Shelton, Editor

Executive Excellence Publishing
1344 East 1120 South
Provo, Utah 84606
phone: (801) 375-4060
fax: (801) 377-5960
web: www.eep.com
e-mail: custserv@eep.com

Ordering Information:
Individual Sales: Executive Excellence Publishing products are available through most bookstores. They also can be ordered directly from Executive Excellence at the address above.

Quantity Sales: Executive Excellence Publishing products are available at special quantity discounts when purchased in bulk by corporations, associations, libraries, and others, or for college textbook/course adoptions. Please write to the address above or call Executive Excellence Publishing Book Sales Division at 1-800-304-9782.

Orders for U.S. and Canadian trade bookstores and wholesalers: Executive Excellence Publishing books and audio tapes are available to the trade through LPC Group/Login Trade. Please contact LPC at 1436 West Randolph Street, Chicago, IL 60607, or call 1-800-626-4330.

ISBN 1-890009-32-6

Printed in the United States of America
10 9 8 7 6 5 4 3 2 1

CONTENTS

Painful Personal Encounters

By Ken Shelton, Editor

*P*ersonal encounters with unethical people and organizations are always painful and often expensive. Beyond reading news stories about hapless souls who are "found out" for some covert activity, have you ever experienced pain and loss first-hand from encounters with unethical people and organizations? Have you, for example, ever been taken by an impersonator, impressionist, impostor, or street-smart pickpocketer? A fraud, fake or forger? One who is more caricature than character? Have you ever invested in such a person or company and felt cheated, victimized, or disillusioned?

The tales are all too common. Even in polite society, the "who's who" has become synonymous with "most wanted," in some cases, dead or alive. Find a list of the "best and worst" in any community and you find a continuum of ethical violations, ranging from innocent indiscretions to sophisticated criminal actions.

Perhaps you can relate to one or more of these cases.

• *Boss.* You apply for employment with a company and are interviewed by a recruiter who presents a very positive picture. You fly in to meet the boss and see for yourself. You want to be open and positive. You accept an offer, even though you have mixed feelings. Still, you believe the business to be above-board. You believe the products and services to be authentic and valuable. But once inside the organization, you find a Mr. Hyde in Dr. Jekyll: You find much that is objectionable about your boss and the company.

• *Teacher.* You enroll in a reputable university and pay expensive tuition and board, only to register for classes taught by absentee professors, graduate assistants, and dead-wood faculty. Even the more popular teachers are often providers of entertainment and easy grades, more actors than academicians. You wonder about the worth of your education and diploma. You become cynical and seek the fastest way out, willingly sacrificing learning for marketable grades and degrees.

• *Politician.* You vote for a man who says all the right things, hits all your political hot buttons, looks good, and seems to have the support of many high-profile people in the community. After the honeymoon year in office, you find him out of touch with the constituency.

• *Minister.* You enjoy the Sunday sermons, but with each passing week, you become more and more disillusioned with your pastor because he doesn't walk his talk or look after the flock. He's passive and distant, removed from reality, pontificating platitudes and telling sentimental stories for emotional effect.

• *Executive.* From a distance, you perceive him to be all powerful. For years, you've been fed a steady diet of propaganda about your corporate leadership, as public relations pumps out reams of press releases and positioning statements. Over time, you learn that most of what appears under his signature he never sees, let alone says; and the closer you get, the more you find discrepancies between policy or principle and practice.

• *Friend.* You're close in proximity and personality. You confide in each other, sharing openly the most intimate and confidential matters of your life with trust and love. But then you discover that your precious words are now being played against you and spoken in derision by others who hear them second hand out of context. You feel betrayed.

As we deal in real time with real people, we are influenced by the externals—personality, voice, face, figure, gesture, clothing, and speech. Unethical people can be very persuasive. Many pass themselves off as real leaders worthy of followers because they are on the screen, on the field, in print, or on the platform. Because they have visibility, we often imbue them with credibility.

High costs. Even on a personal level, when we make mistakes in judgment, the costs can be incredibly high. On a corporate level, the costs of unethical conduct simply boggle the mind; worse, they ruin lives. Several notable news stories document the costs every day. In industry, a captain who is a problem drinker spills thousands of gallons of oil into a pristine bay, causing billions of dollars in damages. In the military, defense secrets are leaked by agents and others who betray national trusts in return for personal favors. In business, executives are caught lying, cheating, and stealing in white-collar crimes that impact an entire department, division, or corporation and waste billions of dollars. In religion, we read of leaders who are exposed for fraud, embezzlement, and quackery. The costs, counted either in lost contributions or in lost faith, are enormous. In government, deceit, waste, and double-dealing cost taxpayers millions of dollars a day. In small and family-owned business, examples are legend of partners (even spouses) cheating each other and becoming bitter enemies over a piece of the action. In families, the incredibly high costs of unethical actions are usually borne by women and children who are left in a disadvantaged position.

One reason unethical behavior is so common is because it can be very rewarding in the short-term. The near-term costs of honest behavior are well documented, making the ethical choice very tough, especially when the long-term payoff or advantage seems remote at best.

Part of the maturation process is to pass through close encounters with unethical people, judging for ourselves who is who and what is what, and then associating with the people and organizations we're most comfortable with. But from cradle to grave, it's "buyer beware." Indeed, along the newly paved "information highway," we see fewer familiar warning signs and symbols. Where visibility means credibility, hitchhikers have the same status as licensed drivers. Anyone with a late-model personal computer—with fax, modem, CD ROM, and a data base—can speed into the market or into a "low barrier to entry" profession and capture share in minutes.

What's Real and Right?

Since media depictions of "real life," both at work and at home, revel in the sordid, and since the "new morality" has all the relativity of the market, many are left wondering what's real, what's right, and where's the truth.

The discontinuity between the real and the ideal, between who we are and how we act at one point in time and who we are and how we act at another point in time, is confusing, both to ourselves and to others. The real (the here and the now) loses all extended meaning, and the ideal (what may be) becomes an impossible dream.

We are all enticed to exchange genuine articles for cheap substitutes, or to trade what's real for what's not. Substitutes are not the real thing, and yet we often buy them, exchanging goodies and toys for girls and boys; fashion and fame for family and fulfillment. As "freshmen" in the college of life, we may succumb to the sweet seductions of appearance and imitation. We may bed with some strange fellows out of naivete. We may go like lambs to certain slaughters. But after an encounter or two, we ought to spot a trend, have the eyes to see certain signs, certain things coming, before we experience them. However, our very goodness, at times, makes us open and trusting, vulnerable to deceit and treachery. So even as adults, we may mistake coins and currency, credentials and character; we may fail to reward the legitimate and then learn to live with sham, fraud, forgery, and deceit.

When one area or aspect of our lives or organizations is more or less legitimate, all other areas then borrow credibility from the Bank of Strength (our strong points). So, we may be highly ethical in one area, highly unethical in another. And when our unethical acts are exposed, our loved ones are typically "stunned" or "shocked," and quick to come to our defense because they know us to be legitimate and lovable in other roles. And yet, we may be based on a solid foundation in a profession only because it imposes a certain discipline on us, meaning we must abide by certain rules and regulations, checks and balances within the system. But once outside that system or specialty, we may register counterfeit to a high degree.

The Gray Scale

Unethical behavior is most often about subtleties, gray areas, whispers, shadows, nuances, and noise. And because of duality in people, differences can be hard to detect. We are all composites, not 100 percent counterfeit or authentic. We are both originals and copies—nurtured from seed and made from scratch in some areas, and influenced by imitation, comparison, or competition in others.

We each have strengths and access to truth, but we also have weaknesses and blind spots. And so difficult judgments and choices must be made daily—not between obvious good and evil, but between people, policies, products, and processes—all reputable to some degree.

There are at least two sides to every person. Seen from different perspectives, we are all polygons. In any given person, one might see pride, arrogance, indifference, aloofness, doubt. And in the same person, others might see just the opposite: humility, compassion, charity, civility, belief. One great obstacle to progress is the thought that we have already arrived. Objective assessment will show that much refining work remains to be done—that many degrees lie beyond the Ph.D. And yet we tend to talk only in extremes and dichotomies—of hell and heaven or of black and white, forgetting that life is color, and an entire scale of gray.

How This Book Is Organized

Ethics is more than just raising questions. Responsible ethics is also about answering questions, taking stands, drawing lines, setting standards, having real penalties for infractions. Even when a society loses respect for law, a well-managed, ethics-oriented organization within that society can maintain a high degree of law and order.

This book is organized around five questions, constituting five sections: 1) Why be ethical? 2) What is ethical judgment? 3) How are ethics applied? 4) What is ethical? Where are ethics practiced? 5) How can we resolve ethical dilemmas?

Our contributing writers represent an impressive collection of leading thinkers and practitioners. I know many of these people personally. I've been in their homes and in their organizations. Although not one is perfect, they are among the best of people—all striving to walk the talk and set a higher standard.

Section I

Why Be Ethical?

Chapter 1

The Cost of Being Ethical

 **By Norman R. Augustine**

What is the one quality that makes a person a "leader"? I have often asked myself that question as I watched friends who are acknowledged leaders—people like Omar Bradley, Jimmy Doolittle, George Bush, Colin Powell, Elizabeth Dole, Wes Unseld, Bill Marriott, and many others.

All the great leaders I've known are very different. But they all have one thing in common: Every great leader puts ethics first. In business, it means putting ethics before profits, before sales, even before staying in business.

Unfortunately, the reputation of business today is that it is an institution not particularly concerned about ethics—and there is some justification for this view. Just a few years ago, we all remember that insider trading was considered a symbol of the way unscrupulous traders "cashed in" on unsuspecting investors. More recently, I read an article that suggested maintaining high ethical standards is simply untenable in the world of business, especially now that we all must compete in a global marketplace where ethical standards vary widely from place to place.

Business, of course, is hardly alone in ethical violations. Shoplifting is up, credit card fraud is up, and escaping one's debts through bankruptcy is up. A news clipping tells of a book store in Boston calling an affiliate in Washington, D.C., in search of the book *Some Honest Men.* Inquiring whether they had *Some Honest Men* in Washington, the clerk was taken aback and then answered, "Perhaps two or three at the most."

Before we let journalism off the hook, let me remind everyone of the media's recent ethical problems, including doctored crash tests, faked photographic exposés, and hidden camera "sting" operations. As Mark Twain is supposed to have observed while discussing his career, "So I became a newspaperman. I hated to do it, but I couldn't find honest employment."

In baseball, we see very public figures, players and owners alike, banished from the game "for life," which under the leagues' curious ethical guidelines, apparently means two or three years. Even among high school and college students, there is disconcerting evidence of unethical behavior. The Josephson Institute of Ethics recently released the results of a survey that showed:

• 39 percent of high school boys and 26 percent of girls say they have stolen something from a store.

• One-fifth of the boys and one-fourth of the girls have stolen something from a family member.

• Two-thirds of high schoolers and one-third of college students have cheated on an exam at least one time.

• One-third of the college-age men and one-fifth of the women say they would lie to get a job.

Now, I personally believe hardly anyone comes to work in the morning—or shows up at school or goes out on the ball field—with the idea of doing something unethical. I believe most people want to be honest and ethical.

But if people set out to do the "right thing," why do so many end up doing something unethical? The answer is that being ethical often —perhaps even usually—entails a short-term cost.

In 1959, Ted Williams was 40 years old and closing out his career with the Boston Red Sox. He was suffering from a pinched nerve in his neck that season. For the first time in his career, he batted under .300, hitting just .254 with 10 home runs. He was the highest salaried player in sports, making $125,000 a year. The following winter, the Red Sox sent him the same contract he had during his disappointing season.

When he got the proposal, Williams sent it back with a note saying that he would not sign it until they gave him the full pay cut allowed. "I was always treated fairly by the Red Sox when it came to contracts," Williams said. "Now they were offering me a contract I didn't deserve. And I only wanted what I deserved." The upshot was that Williams cut his own salary by 25 percent.

Golfers sometimes joke about the player who cheated so regularly that when he once had a "hole in one," he wrote down "zero" on his scorecard. A more admirable approach to ethical behavior on the links was exhibited once during the Kemper Open. The great professional golfer Tom Kite warned his playing partner, Grant Waite, that Waite was about to commit a rules infraction that would cost him two strokes. Waite corrected his behavior, avoided the two-stroke penalty, and went on to win the tournament, eking out a one-stroke victory— over Tom Kite. Not only did Kite lose the victory trophy, he also lost

$94,000 in prize money as a result of coming in second. But he gained a great deal of respect that is far more lasting.

Well, no one ever said being ethical is easy! Being ethical means that we often must substitute short-term gains for a greater, long-term reward.

A century ago, Richard Sears—founder of Sears Roebuck and Company—started the modern mail order industry, supplying a burgeoning nation with innovative products and building a business that gave employment to hundreds of thousands of people.

In his zeal to sell merchandise, Sears occasionally would get carried away with catalogue descriptions, praising products far beyond the literal truth. This in turn led to returned merchandise and reduced profits. But Sears learned his lesson. In later years, he was fond of saying, "Honesty is the best policy. I know because I've tried it both ways."

Martin Marietta, the firm it is my privilege to serve, is staunchly concerned with ethics. The company even keeps track of the number of calls to our "Ethics Hot Line." When the number goes down our Board asks me if we have lost interest in ethics. When it goes up, the Board asks if we have lost ethics! But we still keep track . . . and we learn a lot.

Sometimes the ethical choices people face are relatively easy. Such was the case some time ago when we were in competition for a major government contract, and the day before we were to submit our proposal we received in the mail a copy of our competitor's price sheet. It presumably came from a disgruntled employee of our competitor. Once realizing what we had, the package was promptly handed to our attorneys who informed the government and the competitor what happened. We did not change our bid price.

Incidentally, we lost the contract . . . and some of our employees lost their jobs due to lack of work. By any measure, we paid a heavy price for acting ethically. But I am convinced beyond a question of doubt that it does "pay off" in the long run to be ethical. Martin Marietta has been asked to participate as a partner in any number of projects not only because we have the engineering talent and the technological expertise—but also because we are known as an ethical company.

The truly difficult ethical choices in life involve day-to-day decisions, where the immediate cost is very evident and the long-term "payoff" or advantage seems remote. I am reminded of the Watergate and Iran-Contra scandals, which involved people with no record of wrongdoing who would, under normal circumstances, probably not break the law deliberately. Yet they were drawn into illegality, almost as a boa constrictor consumes its prey.

I labored in the past under the impression that the boa constrictor drops out of a tree on its victims and quickly crushes them in the powerful folds of its body. A quick look in the encyclopedia reveals instead that". . . the snake places two or three coils of its body around the chest of its prey. Then each time the victim exhales its breath the boa simply takes up the slack. After three or four breaths there is no more slack. The prey quickly suffocates and is then swallowed by the boa."

This deadly phenomenon of a victim becoming the unwitting accomplice of its own destruction is not confined to the world of reptiles. Modern life is nothing if not a constant effort to stay one step ahead of the boa.

And that is why I return to the point that there is, in fact, often a short-term cost for acting ethically. I personally believe that is part of the whole ethical equation . . . in fact, it is in some respects the critical part.

I would define the cost of being ethical as similar to the premium we pay for all the meaningful things in our lives. We achieve a college education only at the price of four years of hard work and self-discipline. We enjoy a fulfilling, lifelong marriage only with the sacrifice of some individual preferences and with hard work devoted to truly understanding another person. We are rewarded with a successful business career only after doing more than what is absolutely required. We excel in sports only after many, many hours of training and conditioning. And we achieve greatness as a nation only when we "lose" our ego and devote ourselves to a greater good.

As John Kennedy said about the Apollo program to send men to the moon, "We do these things not because they are easy, but because they are hard."

I believe what needs to be said to our friends, our employees, and our colleagues is that by paying the price of being ethical today, we are actually investing for the longer good. We all know that nothing worth achieving is easily attained. We must not reject ethical behavior because it is hard in the short run, but embrace it for the fact that it yields tremendous dividends over the long run.

And then perhaps, if we can change this perception of ethical behavior, perhaps we will be on our way to a more ethical society. To those who say this is too great a task, that changing a society to be more ethical is impossible, I would point to the story that was once told about the great French Marshal Lyautey, who asked his gardener to plant a certain type of tree. The gardener protested that the tree was slow-growing and would not reach maturity for a hundred years. The Marshal replied, "In that case, there is no time to lose; plant it this afternoon!"

Norman R. Augustine is President and Chief Executive Officer of Lockheed Martin.

Chapter 2

Do Profits and Social Responsibility Mix?

By Charles A. Garfield

*L*evi Strauss patriarch, Walter Haas, Jr., gave a speech to introduce 40 owners of small businesses in Emeryville, California, to the idea of philanthropy. He told his audience:

> Some people argue that doing what's right is somehow contrary to doing what's good for business. I find this view both puzzling and wrong. In my own company, we have learned over and over again that when we do what we believe is proper, the company gains. I don't know how to translate that value into a number that appears on a financial statement, but I do know that we wouldn't want to be in business and we would not be the leader in our industry if we did not enjoy this kind of relationship with our people.

And Frank Tsai of Working Assets points out: "There's no indicator that says you cannot earn equal or better returns on making social investments. Our gross yields are comparable to anybody in money market funds. We wanted to show individuals and institutions that you can promote social change and still make a decent return."

The Body Shop is living proof that a company thoroughly committed to social responsibility can also be a financial success. As Anita Roddick puts it: "We are walking our talk. And still doing okay financially." To say that The Body Shop is "doing okay financially" is a gross understatement. For more than 10 of 15 years that it has been in business, its sales have grown an average of 50 percent a year. In

London financial circles, the Body Shop is referred to as the "shares that defy gravity."

It is not that profits are unimportant to Levi Strauss, Working Assets, The Body Shop, and other socially concerned companies; it's just that they are not the central priority. Says Anita Roddick: "Profits are an integral part (of the business), but you do something more, beyond your own accumulation of material wealth. You do something more which spiritually enhances you or educates you."

Paradoxically, companies that focus on values instead of profits often end up enhancing their profit picture as a result. UCLA business professor, Bill Ouchi, observes that "among the fastest-growing, most profitable major American firms, profits are regarded not as an end in itself nor as the method of keeping score in the competitive process. Rather, profits are the reward to the firm as it continues to provide true value to its customers, to help its employees to grow, and to behave responsibility as a corporate citizen."

Maybe Adam Smith had it backward. There is reason to suggest that companies ensure their own interest by promoting the public interest, rather than the opposite.

In addition to generating monetary rewards, social investments generate less obvious returns. The socially responsible actions of Levi Strauss generate a high level of goodwill. "During our most difficult crisis, when we were closing plants, we had to close one in Arkansas," says Martha Montag-Brown, a former director of community affairs at Levi. "We were a major employer, and it was going to have a big impact on the community. We anticipated negative press. Instead, the paper read: 'Arkadelphia Loses Best Friend.' Every agency in the community offered help and set up services in the plant."

While the effect of such goodwill is hard to quantify, it unquestionably contributes to the firm's financial stability by winning the loyalty of suppliers, retailers, and employees—not to mention the all-important customers, who are becoming increasingly sophisticated shoppers. A poll conducted by Opinion Research Corporation shows that a company's reputation often determines which products 89 percent of adults will buy—and which they will not buy. Not long after the Valdez oil spill, 41 percent of Americans were angry enough to say that they would seriously consider boycotting Exxon. And public pressure forced H. J. Heinz, which sells Starkist tuna, to stop buying tuna harvested in drift nets that also capture dolphins, which drown in their attempts to escape.

Social responsibility also profits companies by enabling them to recruit a high-quality labor force. George Winter writes about the disenchantment of young workers with corporations' lack of environmental concern:

Young people are asking themselves quite seriously what is the point of diligence and hard work. To pollute waste waters even more and to add yet more pollution to the beaches? Why, they wonder, should they get to work on time every morning just to help create more refuse and add more pollution to the community's drinking supplies? Why, they wonder, should they produce high quality work just to generate profits for a factory whose inadequately filtered flue gases are polluting the environment and ruining people's health?

Companies that exhibit socially responsible behavior, that don't require employees to sell their souls in exchange for their paychecks, are rewarded by attracting a more dedicated, loyal, high-quality work force. Patricia Gallup, CEO of PC Connection, believes that the company's social involvement has helped it attract high-caliber employees in an area where unemployment is virtually nil:

The publicity we received in areas such as recycling, historic research, and employee benefits encouraged people to apply to the company. People look at what we are doing and say, "This is the type of company that I would like to be involved with."

There is yet another powerful way in which companies benefit from social responsibility. It has to do not with bottom line, but with the enrichment of the human spirit.

Levi Strauss's Community Involvement Teams consist of employees who volunteer their time to review the needs of the local community, then develop and implement projects to meet those needs. The payoff is not just to the communities that are helped, according to Bob Dunn, the company's vice president for community affairs: "I have seen people whose lives have been transformed. There is much talk about the need out there. We don't focus enough on what people get by doing this work—how it satisfies their need to apply their skills for a useful purpose." In short, giving helps the donor as well as the recipient.

Charles A. Garfield, Ph.D., contributing editor to Executive Excellence, *is the author of* Second to None *and* Peak Performers *and is the president and CEO of The Garfield Group in Redwood City, California.*

Chapter 3

Deterring Dubious Business Behavior

By Alfred A. Marcus

*I*f managers are agents for owners, increasing shareholder wealth is an appropriate way to judge managerial behavior. Negative stock market returns, then, should discourage managers from engaging in dubious behavior. Wise managers will not engage in ethically dubious behavior because of a concern for the possible impact on shareholders.

Indeed, many studies have found abnormal reductions in stock market returns following accusations of bribery, fraud and illegal political contributions as well as after auto recalls, and in the aftermath of major airline accidents. If managers acted as the true agents to their shareholders, they would not allow their companies to fall into predicaments of ethical compromise.

Market Reactions Are Ineffective

These findings raise two issues: 1) the effectiveness of negative stock market returns as a deterrent to ethically dubious behavior; and 2) the appropriateness of relying on stockholder returns to deter managers from engaging in dubious behavior. Enlightened self-interest may not be a sufficient guarantee that ethical behavior will take place; a stronger ethical stance, one which is not tied to pure self-interest, may be needed.

• *Effectiveness.* If shareholder returns are to deter dubious corporate behavior, managers must be aware that shareholders are likely to react negatively to announcements of dubious corporate conduct. But how strong is the signal that shareholders send to managers, and how capable are managers of perceiving the negative reaction that springs from shareholder interests?

To estimate the impact of their dubious acts on stock prices, managers may 1) combine the market reaction over time and across companies; 2) combine the market responses by company, time period, or both; and 3) assess the market reaction on a case-by-case basis. The first perspective assumes that managers perceive the market's reaction to be stable across time and companies. The best estimate of the effect of dubious acts is thus the average effect for a large number of companies over a long period. For this perspective to deter dubious acts, managers must be aware of the abnormal returns for a portfolio of firms that have engaged in dubious activities.

Managers, however, may not want to rely on the aggregate results, as these can be misleading. For example, if the market's reaction to dubious behavior differs across time or companies, managers may decide that only the effects for a particular time period or a particular company are relevant, and may not pay attention to the overall pattern. Their concern, appropriately, would be with the market response to their company, or to their company in a given period of time. For the stock market to dependably discourage dubious behavior, managers would have to consider the market reactions for a specific company or companies and specific time periods.

Managers may be mainly concerned with behavior that is closely related to their role and function. Their view of the world may encompass only a minute fraction of the relevant information. For instance, if they work on product development or manufacturing, they will participate directly only in a handful of decisions, observe results of only a few of them, and are likely to perceive stock market reactions on a case-by-case basis.

Indeed, anecdotal evidence suggests that managers view stock market returns in a piecemeal manner, that they are incapable of seeing the big picture and dismiss evidence they should take into account. Because some managers focus on a few isolated examples, they conclude that the stock market is an unreliable indicator of corporate performance. Because of selective perception, there is no guarantee that shareholder returns can discourage dubious behavior.

• *Appropriateness.* The classic theory of the firm emphasizes the stock market valuation of the company. It is an investor's model. Nonetheless, it typically has been qualified to read that the responsibility to earn profits for shareholders is bounded by the claims of laws and ethics. Thus, serving shareholder interests, if properly understood, can be consistent with other claims so long as the interests of shareholders are not violated by paying attention to these other claims.

New Standard Needed

A different ethical standard, derived from religious sources such as the Sermon on the Mount or from philosophical ones such as

Immanual Kant's formulation of the categorical imperative, would demand an unconditional devotion to what is "right" regardless of shareholder interests. If shareholder interests conflict with other claims, then the needs of shareholders would have to be sacrificed.

In truth, one can readily imagine situations facing managers where shareholder returns will conflict with ethical standards. Under these circumstances, shareholder reaction is an inducement not a deterrent to dubious activity. Shareholder returns tell managers to do one thing; ethical standards tell them to do another—and it is up to the managers to decide. They have to choose which interest to favor—that of their shareholders or that of their ethical conscience—and nothing tells them how to reconcile the conflicts between ethics and profits.

Managers will face situations that require them to adopt a more rigorous ethical standard that may be at odds with the interest of shareholders. When facing these situations, managers must ignore stockholders and put these other considerations first. They cannot simply rely on shareholder returns as a guide to their actions.

Beyond Self-Interest

The stock market often punishes managers that behave in an ethically dubious manner. However, the stock market is not always ethically deterrent. First, there is the matter of managerial perception. If the stock market punishes managers who violate ethical norms and rewards managers who conform to them, managers' awareness of the signals that the market sends has to be sufficiently clear to influence the actions they take. However, despite the importance of the market to managers, managerial awareness of the impact of their actions on the market may not be sufficiently clear for the market to be an effective deterrent. This is because there are alternatives, equally valid ways of assessing the market returns. Moreover, the attention of managers with respect to these returns may be selective so that it is hard for them to connect the policies they carry out to shareholder interests.

The market cannot be relied upon to always act in accord with generally accepted ethical doctrines. There will be instances when it rewards dubious conduct and punishes virtuous behavior. In these instances, it is not an appropriate guide to managerial action. Rather, it leads managers astray and draws them from their basic moral duties. These considerations suggest that society needs to go beyond self-interest and prudence in assuring that managers keep from committing morally dubious acts.

The stock market, in short, is not a dependable deterrent to dubious behavior. Even if 95 percent of the time, it punishes those that stray from ethical responsibility or it rewards those that stick to their moral principles, there still are the remaining 5 percent of the cases where managers have to decide where to place their allegiance. These instances raise fundamental issues because fiduciary duty is an important one, both legally and ethically. It is not one that should be treated lightly or with disrespect. Yet in these instances, adhering to moral principle would have to come at the expense of the managers' fiduciary duties.

The only dependable deterrent to dubious behavior is moral duty, an awareness of the consequences of one's actions and an attention to right conduct. The meaning here is that managers should treat people in the organization and those outside of it with respect, as ends and not as means, as Kant has stated it, and as autonomous creatures not subject to managerial coercion. These standards should apply regardless of the short- or long-term shareholder impact.

Stockholders should not necessarily be the sole determinant of "goodness" of a particular policy. If the rational pursuit of self-interest always comes before moral duty, then humanity is the great loser.

Alfred A. Marcus teaches courses in business and government at the Carlson School of Management, University of Minnesota.

Chapter 4

A Price for Principle

By David L. Neidert

Building is costly. Architects, designers, contractors, meeting-after-meetings—all of these elements add to the cost of any project. Every cost aspect of building is detailed to give those investing an idea about their return-on-investment, the risk to capital they will invest, and the consequences if commitments are not made and deadlines met.

As with building, principle, too, has a price. Integrity, truthfulness, and character demand that we count the cost. Building principle into our lives requires we calculate the cost before we find ourselves in the intensity of the fray. With no inner foundation of commitment to principle, public displays of character will fade in the heat of life's conflicts, as surely as grass will wither in a desert's sun.

A Call to High Standards

Integrity, honesty, truth, justice—universally high standards—demand we live to their requirements, not compromise them to our needs. These principles do not change with time, but remain beacons to which we are drawn. It is vital that we count the cost of following principle, least we find ourselves unable to fulfill the qualities that these virtues demand.

Counting the cost of principle and building on that cost happens over time. Building principle that can withstand life's storms is constructed brick-by-brick. Living a life of principle means a commitment of the will, a willingness to stand firm in what is right, even in the smallest of daily issues.

The cost of living up to the ultimate high call to principle may never happen to us. But because we live in a complex global society, we may be confronted by instances in which we must remain true to principle above all else. Living by principles may ask us to risk it all—our careers, fortune, material possessions, family, prestige—for the sake of what is right and true over what is expedient and easy.

Counting the cost of principle beforehand may indeed place us at the moment-of-truth when principle must win over personal gain. Epictetus, the 1st century A.D. philosopher, gives us advice in counting the cost. "In every affair consider what precedes and follows, and then undertake it. Otherwise, you will begin with spirit; but not having thought of the consequences, when some of them appear you will shamefully desist. Consider first what the matter is, and what your nature is able to bear."

An Ultimate Price

The price of principle may never cost us personal loss. But principle may, at times, demand every cent we have invested. The lives of Nelson Mandela, of Abraham Lincoln and of the great social reformer Mahatma Gandhi let us know that imprisonment—and even death—may be the price of principle. Charles Swindoll writes about costs in his best-selling book, *Strengthening Your Grip*. Swindoll reminds us that the fight for principle—for truth, integrity and justice—cannot be fought by "weary, ill-trained, noncommitted, half-hearted troops." The war of principle will be won in the long run by those who are willing to pay the price for principle, even if the cost is life itself.

Counting the cost of principle and living them out must happen in every waking moment. Living by principle is not a once-in-a-while venture, but an all-of-the-time choice.

Building is costly. Wise is the person who counts the cost of principle and is willing, in daily life, to pay the price for building a solid personal foundation. And when the rains fall and the floods come and the winds beat upon our building of principle, we will stand firm.

David Neidert is the director of auxiliary services at Anderson University, Anderson, Indiana.

Chapter 5

Reinforcing Ethics in a Recession

By David Perry

*I*nitiatives in ethics suffer when executives regard such efforts as extras or investments to be postponed in tough times. During a recession, consumer confidence is low, and business failures are up, credit tightens, and pressures mount. Company survival and job security can become the overwhelming focus in business decision-making, pushing employee and management concerns for ethical conduct into the background, and putting enormous strains on a company's operating values.

This is not to say, however, that recessions alone can be blamed for business misconduct. The Wall Street insider trading scandals and the savings and loan frauds were not due to recessionary pressures. Even normal business constraints and misplaced incentives can strain a company's operating values, rendering it vulnerable to misconduct. But a recession can greatly magnify potential risk areas.

What Can Happen

Recessionary pressures manifest themselves in many areas: corner-cutting in production; "creative" accounting; no-holds-barred marketing and sales practices; and high-pressure purchasing techniques, and in the conduct of layoffs and RIFs (reductions in force). RIFs generate employee grievances and resentment. Who to lay off is probably the most agonizing decision a manager can face. But a RIF is a strong test of whether ethics has truly become imbedded in the corporate culture.

If employees see that the RIF leaves unscathed an "old boy network" in management, if they see their retirement benefits cut, or if they see that ethics "whistleblowers" are among the first to be let go, employees will be unlikely to take seriously any future company statements on business ethics.

Some U.S. firms have already taken these concerns to heart, making sincere efforts to cushion the effects of layoffs and to see that RIF decisions are made in responsible ways. A few go the second mile, offering counseling and workshops on resume writing and job interviewing, and even running full-page ads in local papers notifying other firms of the availability of valuable potential hires who lost their jobs.

During recessionary periods, managers need to ask: Would my employees say that management "walks its talk" even in tough times? Would our customers and suppliers say the same?

What Can Be Done?

Three things can be done.

• *First, management should take a critical view of the organization to assess risks and vulnerabilities.* If the company already has an existing ethics program, now is a good time to take its measure. What's working, and what's not?

Consider using interviews, focus groups, questionnaires, and ethics-related questions to existing employee surveys. Employees should be asked about their perceptions of key operating values and their attitudes toward the company and its management. In addition, an assessment should determine whether employees have the skills to identify and adequately address ethics issues that they may face in their daily work environment.

Systems that function well during economic growth can often become inadvertent contributors to unethical conduct during tough times. For example, a MBO performance evaluation system can effectively disperse rewards to the greater contributors in boom times. But in a recession, not hitting the numbers may mean the possible loss of one's job, not just a smaller bonus, putting extreme pressure on employees. These incentives and pressures should also be probed in an assessment.

• *Second, management may wish to refocus on the company's traditional core values, perhaps to develop or refine a "credo" or short statement of those values.* This effort can provide a template against which strategic plans and short-term goals can be consciously compared. It can also send an important signal to employees that the company doesn't intend to sacrifice its basic principles, even in the face of extraordinary bottom-line demands.

Credos alone, however, may not be enough. Many corporations have also developed more detailed codes of ethical conduct, realizing that broad statements of values may be insufficient to guide employee actions in "gray" areas. For example, under what circumstances can employees gather and utilize competitor intelligence? A new employee recruited from a competitor? The best corporate codes don't simply specify prohibited actions in dry, legalistic fashion; they provide explanations or rationales of important rules of conduct and illustrate how company standards apply in particular situations. Areas of greatest potential risk should be addressed through these guidelines. If a company already has an adequate code of ethics, then employee knowledge of the standards (and their attitudes and perceptions of operating values) can be assessed.

• *Third, companies need to reinforce ethics standards in formal training and informal discussions within departments and work groups.* Companies may wish to use in-house training staff or outside professionals. Involve supervisors in the leadership of the program, perhaps "teaming" with professional trainers. Direct supervisors can provide credible, detailed answers on ethics issues that "go with the territory" in their specific job functions. This can also serve to encourage employees to bring concerns to their supervisors without embarrassment or fear.

When the supervisor is the cause of an employee's concern, or when an employee is unable to obtain a satisfactory response to a valid concern, companies need to provide alternative channels for employees to obtain advice and raise questions on matters of corporate ethics. Human Resources, Legal, and Security are obvious channels for certain questions. But U.S. firms are increasingly creating a separate channel for matters of corporate misconduct, variously titled "ethics ombudsman," "business conduct officer," etc. Individuals chosen to fill this role need to be highly regarded within the company for their integrity, confidentiality, and counseling skills.

These efforts must be backed by thorough investigations of allegations of misconduct, and by consistent discipline of proven misconduct. If management hammers those who raise concerns in good faith, or if it winks at the misconduct of top performers or those who are "politically" well-connected, cynicism will result. The "ethics officer" can initiate investigations, but in most cases he or she may need to touch base with a high-level "ethics committee," composed of Legal, HR, Internal Audit, and senior management to decide how to proceed. The "ethics officer" should ensure that investigations move to closure and that confidentiality and due process are upheld throughout.

The Outlook

Corporate initiatives in ethics suffer in tough economic times when executives regard such efforts as "extras," as investments that don't show immediate returns and can be postponed until the company can better "afford to be ethical." This way of thinking is shortsighted. Ethics is not a box that can be checked after every employee has been through an ethics training program or has acknowledged reading the code of conduct. Ethics has to do with the basic culture and operating values of an organization—the pride and satisfaction employees find in their work, the attention to quality in production, the degree to which suppliers and customers are treated fairly and honestly—all of which impinge on the company's overall reputation and success. These matters are too vital to be ignored in the best of economic times, but especially when a recession threatens to expose the darker side of a company's culture.

David Perry is a consultant in advisory services with the Ethics Journal.

Chapter 6

A Question of Ethics

By Barbara Strandell

We have all seen the scathing indictments of public figures in the media; their mismanagement of others' money has called their business ethics into question. As one watches this from afar, one can't help but wonder that indeed there might be something wrong in a system that allows such behavior to go unchecked until it reaches the million or billion dollar mark. And then we go back to our corporate jobs, feeling stressed and ripped off by the little acts of treachery of which we have become victims, without the media or courts noticing.

Thousands of managers victimize their employees everyday and never get caught. Those managers and executives contribute to the stress and unhappiness of millions of workers who want only to do their jobs and receive fair treatment in the process.

There is an implicit social contract that management of our large publicly held corporations have with shareholders, customers, and employees. Many corporate mission statements make those social contracts explicit. For the shareholders, there are promises of adequate and growing financial returns; for the customers, there are commitments to providing competitively priced, high quality products and services; and for the employees, we often see words that imply the corporation will be sensitive to their general welfare. Corporations are notorious for claiming that "people" are their greatest asset.

The social contract with employees is being broken. Thus, this "great asset" is currently experiencing record levels of work-related stress.

To understand why this contract has gone awry, merely look under the satin sheets of the corporate culture: management negligence creates a continuous deterioration of morale, pride, and loyalty.

Layoffs, acquisitions, and divestitures obviously have a serious impact on the "survivors." But the real disease is the on-going management practices that alienate and suffocate people on a daily basis. Consider a few of these practices:

• Asking all employees to take "time off without pay" over the holidays, because the "numbers" are not coming in as planned—when people know that management has misrepresented business results and forecasts. The impact: unfair punishment.

• Requiring employees to sit through dead-end meetings because the executive in charge can't make a decision or doesn't trust people to do their jobs. The impact: helplessness.

• Conducting weekly meetings where the boss spends hours reading memos to people and delegating follow-up. The impact: disrespect.

• Implementing contests that eat up precious time and energy for the sake of an executive's ego. The impact: misuse of time and money.

• Using exclusionary language, such as military or sexual metaphors and analogies. The impact: alienation.

• Using company resources to remodel the homes, cabins, or vacation condominiums of executives. The impact: deception.

• Promoting individuals mid-year who are not performing, but who are friends of a higher level executive, and all the employees know that the "good old boy network" is operating! The impact: no link between performance and reward.

• Providing retired or "golden parachute" class executives with lucrative consulting contracts in the midst of hiring freezes, and policies that ban merit increases. The impact: anger and frustration.

These and other management practices erode the confidence of the corporate employee and contribute to the cycles of stress and malaise that have become widespread in the corporate world. Even if upper management doesn't take these ethical breaches seriously, the marketplace will! Alienation of a workforce ultimately impacts a company's ability to compete and achieve their profit objectives.

Many employees are unhappy with their work, but unable to bail out; so they hang in there, with resentment toward the company, working at about half of their potential pace. They often "act out" by abusing the system the way they feel they have been abused; ultimately, they burn out, making worklife even more miserable for those around them. The net result is a less productive workforce.

So the obvious "big bad guys" are getting caught; some of the "smaller bad guys" are getting bought off by new management; and many employees are finding ways out of the corporate system. It will take a massive leap in consciousness before we see more nurturing, respectful, ethical behaviors in the management culture.

Barbara Strandell worked many years for Fortune 500 *companies before "dropping out" to become a consultant and author based in St. Paul, Minnesota.*

Chapter 7

Ethics Aren't Optional

By Warren Bennis

Alas, there seem to be no innocents left in America. Ollie North claims to be a patriot, but his patriotism has resulted in a home security system and a numbered Swiss bank account. Teenagers peddle drugs on the streets in East Los Angeles. Self-proclaimed men of God recite the Ten Commandments on Sundays and break them the other six days of the week. Spying for dollars is our latest growth industry, and Wall Street looks more and more like a branch of Sing Sing. In the late 1960s, yippies were political activists. In the 1980s, yippies are young indicted professionals, while yuppies, our grand acquisitors, consumed by consumption, turn out to be unindicted professionals— those who haven't got caught yet.

Young children are pushed into boutique nursery schools, where excellence is measured by the cut of one's Polo shirt. Teenagers drive SUVs and BMWs, and are pressured to score stupendously on their SATs so they can go to Stanford with Chelsea Clinton or to Brown with Amy Carter and Cosima Von Bulow, and graduate to investment banking where the players use real money and jail is the only limit.

Kids no longer dream of going to the moon, or making a better mousetrap. They dream of money and they know that the best things in life are VCRs, cellular telephones, Beemers, dinner at the Quilted Giraffe or Rebecca's. They don't vote, of course, believing that politics are obsolete, along with politicians.

President Bill Clinton made himself obsolete by denying that he was a womanizer, then womanizing and claiming he hadn't. When faced with further evidence of his womanizing, he and Hilary denied everything and resorted to "executive privilege." The American people seemed as confused as Clinton himself as to what he did wrong. Was he under fire because he allegedly committed adultery or because he allegedly lied? Or was he simply guilty of bad judgment?

The hippest citizens dismissed the charges of both adultery and lying, because after all everyone who is anyone does both.

Our national confusion over Clinton's alleged mistakes vividly demonstrates a startling ethical decline. More and more we are unable to identify or define what constitutes unethical behavior.

After the penultimate Wall Street trader Ivan Boesky was nailed, a TV news crew went into a Wall Street bar and interviewed some young traders. Each and every one expressed admiration for Boesky and contempt for the Security and Exchange Commission. Earlier, when four of their own were caught playing games that were too fast and loose even for Wall Street, the disgraced young traders were more censured than pitied. Winning isn't everything; it's the only thing—and getting caught is for losers. And, as one market analyst said, it isn't a bull market or a bear market, "it's a pig market."

After another round of arrests on the Street, an investment banker told the *New York Times* that the sight of their colleagues in handcuffs "put the fear of God in everybody." Such late-inning invocations are, of course, S.O.P. for white-collar felons, as we saw in the wake of Watergate. And why not? Almost anyone would rather wear a halo than handcuffs. But, as the revelations about Jim and Tammy Baker and their PTL (Praise the Lord) Club show, the church is no holier than Wall Street, and is at least as profitable.

Ollie North's exercise in patriotism for profit, the games other White House notables play, Wall Street's dirty dozen, Hart's fall, are manifestations of an enormous social crisis.

In this highly materialistic nation, the prevailing ethic is, at best, pragmatic, and, at worst, downright dishonest. It's every man for himself, and never mind God, country, or anything else. There seems to be no such thing as the common good or the public interest. Only self-interest. That old entrepreneurial spirit is running amuck, and the country is coming unstuck.

Ted Turner buys MGM and guts it. GE gobbles up RCA while the airlines feed on each other. TV evangelists squeeze big bucks out of believers, and Wall Street traders and Washington patriots pedal their services to the highest bidders. The rich get richer, and the poor get poorer. And the federal deficit gets bigger. As the poet William Butler Yeats said in another time and place, "the center is not holding."

It is time, then, to face this ethical deficit. Ethics and conscience aren't optional. They are the glue that binds society together—the quality in us that separates us from cannibals. Without conscience and ethics, talent and power amount to nothing.

Warren Bennis is a distinguished Professor of Business Administration and founding chairman of the Leadership Institute at the University of Southern California. He is the author of Managing People is Like Herding Cats.

Chapter 8

Managing by Values

 **By Ken Blanchard**

When I talk about *Fortunate 500* companies, people smile. Even before they know what it means, they feel they would like to work for such a company. They also sense that few presently exist. A *Fortunate* 500 company is one determined by: The quality of life available to its employees; the quality of service provided to its customers; and the quality of its products and their placement in the marketplace. If a company does these things, I feel the hard numbers of sales revenues and profitability will directly follow.

In a book that I co-authored with Michael O'Connor entitled *Managing by Values,* we explain how an organization can become a *Fortunate* 500 company by learning how to define, communicate, and align their values with their practices.

1. Identifying core values. Managing by values begins by identifying a core set of operating values. Many companies claim they have a set of core values, but what they mean is a list of generic business beliefs that everyone would agree with—such as having integrity, making a profit, responding to customers, etc. Such values have meaning only when they are further defined in terms of how people actually will behave and are rank-ordered to reveal priority.

For example, Disney's core values for their theme parks are, in order of importance, safety, courtesy, the show (performing according to the requirements of your particular role), and efficiency. If these values weren't so carefully ordered, people would be left to their own devices. For example, a bottomline-oriented manager might overemphasize efficiency and thus jeopardize higher-ranking values.

Today's economy calls for a new approach that builds on the foundation of an effective organization—namely, its mission and its values. Rather than focus solely on results, *Fortunate* 500 companies first emphasize values—the beliefs, attitudes, and feelings that top management has about employees, customers, quality, ethics, integrity, social responsibility, growth, stability, innovation, and flexibility.

An organization today must know what it stands for and on what principles it operates. No longer is values-based behavior an interesting philosophical choice—it is a requisite for survival.

Once an organization has a clear picture of its mission and values, it has a strong basis for evaluating its management practices and bringing them into alignment with the articulated mission and values.

2. Communicating core values. This step involves making sure that your values are evident to all stakeholders—employees, customers, suppliers, stockholders, and the community. The core values of Norstan, a telecommunications company headquartered in Minneapolis, Minnesota, are found in the adjectives *Ethical, Responsive, Profitable,* in that order. The company then operationalized these values in terms of their major stakeholders, which they distributed to all employees:

• *With Customers:* Anticipating customer needs and servicing them responsively. Providing state-of-the-art products and services of highest quality.

• *With Employees:* Creating a fulfilling environment that attracts and motivates the most talented people. Offering a quality work experience that anticipates employee needs and helps them to be productive to their maximum potential.

• *With Shareholders:* Maintaining a strong growth rate and return on shareholder investment. Achieving a significant market position in the areas we serve. Any opportunity that arises for Norstan to trumpet its values, it seizes upon. For example, these values appear on framed posters throughout the company's corporate headquarters and regional facilities, every business card highlights them, as well as corporate brochures and reports.

3. Aligning values and practices. Once the top management of a company has articulated the values the corporation wants to exemplify, and they have been broadly communicated, the final step is to see if these values are actually practiced in day-today operations. This step represents about 80 percent of the *Managing by Values* effort. To be effective, values and strategies need to bring together the energies of all people, especially those people dealing with the company's various publics. Without some method of identifying gaps between values and behavior, a set of core values is nothing more than a wish list.

Inherent in our concept of a *Fortunate* 500 company is having the behavior of the leaders aligned with the key corporate values. That is, is management "walking its talk"? For example, if top management indicates that they value innovation and flexibility but then they have an authoritarian-based bureaucracy with excessive layers of management that discourages flexibility and fluidity in decision-making—there is an alignment problem.

Or if top management says that they value the full development of employees' potential but then the company has a performance review system that forces managers to rate their people on a normal distribution curve, in which only a few people can "win," again, there is an alignment problem.

Holt Companies, a producer and distributor of heavy equipment engines for the construction and energy industries based in San Antonio, Texas, provides a good example of how the values/practices alignment can work. Holt found that following the steps of the *Managing by Values* process led to many frank discussions among top management, which included feedback to the CEO, Peter Holt.

"It was very uncomfortable," admits Holt. "I was forced to confront the gaps between what I thought about myself and how others perceived me. I had always thought I had an inspirational style, but it turned out I had only been inspiring myself!"

Holt's desire to transform himself and improve the working environment for all of his employees lead to a shift in priorities.

"As a result of those initial meetings, Peter admitted he had been placing too much emphasis on growth for growth's sake and not enough on stability," comments Barney Fitton, general parts manager at Holt of Ohio Company in Columbus. "But, after listening to us, he was willing to change so that we could focus on long-term, controlled growth and build stronger relationships with our employees and our customers."

In companies where there is a high degree of alignment between key values and practices around customers and employees, financial results that stockholders desire will follow. Why? Because misalignment between values and practices creates an energy drain that sabotages productive behavior, as customers and employees are continually confronted with incongruity between announced values and practiced values. Alignment liberates energy and empowers people with shared value systems to act congruently. That makes for loyal customers and employees and a productive environment.

Seven Steps to Start the Journey

We envision seven steps to help a company become one of the *Fortunate* 500. The first five steps involve diagnosis; the last two steps involve implementation.

1. Articulate values. Top management needs to establish a clear set of values that they want the organization—and its employees—to represent. This would include specific descriptions of what each value would look like in practice on a daily basis and a methodology for measuring each practice on an on-going basis. For example, if one of the desired values is "outstanding customer service," on a daily basis this value might be seen in employees going out of their way to help customers, perhaps in doing things beyond what is required.

2. Identify and describe key practices. Key practices then need to be assessed to determine a baseline of current business operations. This information would come from a variety of methods, including interviews, historical documents, observation of operational meetings, and so on.

3. Compare values with practices. The extent and nature of alignment or misalignment between the stated values and actual practices is then determined. Helpful in this step is additional information from focus groups, employee and customer surveys, as well as analysis of practices compared with the experience of other companies.

4. Establish priorities for realignment. Issues and priorities regarding alignment of practices with stated values are then itemized. Changes deemed to have the greatest impact are scheduled to be made first.

5. Recommend changes and implementation strategy. The required changes are defined and integrated with one another to create a vision of how the company would be run based on today's information, products, and markets and with a process for continual change as new information or priorities dictate. An implementation strategy and timeline are then developed.

6. Make desired changes. Alignment changes are made with care being taken that they are effectively integrated with existing practices. This requires the combined and managed efforts of many people over the years. Involvement of people is a key to build commitment. Outside expertise may be helpful in specific areas, such as business planning, management training, performance management, team building, customer responsiveness, compensation, and reward systems.

7. Monitor progress. A process for measuring on-going performance and progress is developed and installed. An effective monitoring system helps maintain the appropriate degree of involvement by employees at all levels and alerts management to the need for mid-course corrections as they are needed.

Ken Blanchard is Chairman of Blanchard Training and Development, Inc., in San Diego, California, and co-author with Michael O'Connor of Managing by Values.

Chapter 9

Ethical Leadership

By Willard G. Butcher

*I*n addressing this difficult topic, I wish to be neither too general, nor too specific. Nor, too pontifical. But I can make no promises. It is said about General Robert E. Lee, "He preached oh so gently, but nonetheless he still preached."

My topic is the decline of ethical behavior. My own perspective on "ethics" is, by definition, that of a businessman. But whether or not you aspire to business, my message is the same: ethical behavior and effective leadership are intertwined and inseparable.

Meaningful leadership—leadership that in the long run counts for something—cannot be accompanied by moral collapse. The leader who acts ethically will ultimately succeed. The leader who lacks in ethical foundation will ultimately fail.

A spot check of the landscape indicates that something is terribly wrong with our ethics. I would argue that the principle cause is the maelstrom of change. Rarely have times been more turbulent.

In periods of upheaval, people cut loose from their moorings, and thus lose their bearings. And when you combine this with today's appalling lack of historical perspective, you see why some among us have forgotten who we are and what we ought to stand for—thus, the recent avalanche of ethical abuses in cutting corners, in bending rules, in cheating.

On Wall Street, insider trading scandals have converted Phi Beta Kappa graduates of the finest business schools into convicted felons. In government, shocking disclosures at all levels—from the Iranian crisis in Washington to municipal payoffs in New York—call into question the ethical standards of government leaders.

And even in the pristine halls of academia, embarrassing revelations of rule-breaking in amateur athletics have caused commentator George Will to label some leading universities as "schools for scandal."

While all of this is most disturbing, such breaches of ethics are not new. Ethical abuses have been with us from the beginning. Often, "doing wrong" has been a shortcut to "making good."

So why, you may ask, should we be overly concerned abut the current crop of ethical abuses? Well, as the British diplomat who urgently cabled back to London put it, "The gravity of the situation here is impossible to exaggerate—but I'll try!"

I am concerned that today's attitude toward ethics reflects a "graver" situation than in the past. "Graver" because in many cases the abusers themselves either won't acknowledge or can't understand that they have done anything wrong. "Everyone does it," they say. "And besides, our lawyers will get us off." "Graver" because ethical abusers often are treated more like celebrities than pariahs. And "Graver" too because the average citizen today has almost become inured to such behavior. People are starting to accept ethical abuse as the societal norm. As comedienne Lily Tomlin says, "No matter how cynical you become, it's never enough to keep up"!

And it's this cynicism that is most alarming. To quote an old aphorism, "How can I trust a man not to lie—when I know I would lie in his place." We will never rid ourselves of ethical abuse until we first reject categorically the notion that ethics today just aren't very important.

In business, the emphasis is on making a quick buck. The "new business order," the *Times* tells us, "eschews loyalty to workers, products, structure, business, factories, communities, even the nation. All such allegiances are viewed as expendable under the new rules. With survival at stake, only market leadership, strong profits, and a high stock price can be allowed to matter."

High premiums are paid today not particularly for quality service on long-term building of a business but rather for making money quickly, getting rich, and getting out. And that's wrong.

What I care about is that society condemns unacceptable conduct to the point that a would-be ethical violator will forever be an outcast.

In education, we have started to lose sight of the reasons schools were built in the first place—to teach values and to promote scholarship. As one college president said tongue-in-cheek, "We're trying to build a university that our football team can be proud of!" Gallows humor to be sure, but a chilling indicator of how far in the wrong direction the educational pendulum has swung. Former Education Secretary Bill Bennett has suggested that all universities ought to teach ethics in a serious way—not just with a course or two, but with a comprehensive program.

We seem to have lost sight of the fact that there are fundamental rights and wrongs. And I agree that these precepts need to be reinforced to students. Indeed, the occasional inspirational speaker who gives students what someone once labeled, "the equivalent of a quick dunk in a morality bath," simply won't suffice anymore.

Beyond formal classwork in ethics, colleges also must take more of a stand on ethical issues, particularly those in their own backyard. All too often, a university is more willing to deal with moral issues that have little local relevance rather than confront issues of more immediate concern on its own campus.

We need to reassert the importance and urgency of making decisions in an ethical way. Ethical decision-making isn't an option today. It's an obligation—in business, in education, in government, in our daily lives.

For example, my own company, like most others, has a Code of Conduct—a blueprint that spells out the value standards we expect our employees to live up to. But having a written document is no guarantee that decisions will be made in an ethical way. We must constantly work at making our Code of Conduct a "living document" and the practice of corporate ethics, a "living spirit" in the organization.

Stated another way, "Church on Sunday, sin on Monday" ethics will not cut it. We must practice what we preach and incorporate ethics into every decision we make.

Now, I doubt seriously that anyone aspires to be a convicted felon. On the contrary, I suspect that most people aspire to be leaders. At some time, you will likely get your chance. What standards will you adhere to? What principles will you embrace? What values will you practice yourselves and instill in your coworkers?

Let me suggest a point of departure. Michael Novak, an eminent scholar at the American Enterprise Institute, has said, "The fundamental motive of democratic capitalism—to produce greater well-being for the world's people—is, at base, a moral motive." I agree.

Despite what some may argue, the primary responsibility of business is much more than simply using resources to engage in activities to increase profits. Profits, to be sure, are critical. You won't live long if you have air to breathe tomorrow but none today. And if a business intends to be around for the long term, it must make profits in the short term as well. But profits alone are not the answer.

Forty years ago, I received some simple advice that has stayed with me from a family friend named Marion Folsom, the architect of our nation's social security system and then a top executive of the Eastman Kodak Company.

"Bill," Mr. Folsom said, "you're going to find that 95 percent of all decisions you'll ever make in your career could be made as well by any reasonably intelligent high school sophomore. But they'll pay you for the other five percent."

And it's those five percent, that will be the most difficult—the subjective 51-49 decisions that will call into play your own long-term vision, your corporate ideals, the discipline and constancy of your character.

If, in making these decisions, you rely on clear ethical principles, a firm commitment toward ethical behavior, and an inflexible standard of what's right and wrong, then your track record will be very good.

Moreover, if you use such personal standards to set corporate standards—you will exemplify the kind of leadership that seems in such short supply today. Leaders like Reg Jones at General Electric, Irving Shapiro at DuPont, and David Rockefeller, my predecessor at Chase, rightfully saw their responsibilities extending beyond quarterly profit statements and into areas of broader public policy and societal concern.

Or a leader like John Shad, who has battled corruption as chairman of the Securities and Exchange Commission and was the prime mover behind a program at the Harvard Business School to make the study of ethics an integral part of the curriculum. Or a leader like Jim Burke, the chairman of Johnson & Johnson, who, when faced with the sabotaging of its largest consumer product, immediately removed Tylenol from the shelves. As costly as that decision was, Burke never hesitated. Johnson & Johnson had developed a tradition over decades for integrity. And that tradition stood it well in its moments of crisis. When Jim Burke asked the American people to trust him, they did just that.

So too will they trust you if you lead in a way that clearly indicates that at your business, "Ethics is spoken here."

Business leaders today can't shrink from their obligations to set a moral example for those they lead. They must draw the line between on the one hand, the perpetual push for higher profits and on the other, actions antagonistic to the values of society.

Put another way, ethical business leadership requires not only harvesting the fruit we can pluck today; not only investing in the small trees and experimental hybrids that won't yield a thing in this quarter or the next, but also caring for the soil that allows us to produce such a rich harvest in the first place.

Today's painful headlines coming out of our counting houses and our court houses remind us that ethical standards are not monuments, but living ideals. They thrive and wither as our commitment to them waxes and wanes.

Mature people who aspire to leadership must begin to grapple much more meaningfully with this issue of ethical standards. They must consistently work at it and instill its importance in others. If we do, I am confident that we will become the kind of responsible leaders that we so desperately need.

Willard C. Butcher is retired chairman of the Chase Manhattan Corporation.

Chapter 10

Can We Afford Ethics?

By Gifford and Elizabeth Pinchot

*E*thics is no longer a luxury—it is a staple in the success of any enterprise. In times of global limits and global competition, we can no longer rely on growth and plentiful cheap resources to solve our problems. We face a familiar dilemma: Do we need more control or more freedom? More soft humanism and equality, or more hard discipline and sacrifice? More individual risk and initiative, or more collective collaboration? It can be tempting to hunker down in the midst of extensive lay-offs and business failures, foolish though we know it to be. We wish for predictability, hope for wise control from the center, and feel coerced to manage things for the short-term bottom line. And yet we know the bureaucratic solution no longer works—designed for defense, to resist change, and concentrate intelligence and control in the head. More open self-organizing systems, modeled on nature and free enterprise systems of multiple small entrepreneurships, have a capacity for self-renewal that is more than self-preservation.

These lessons are not lost on giants such as IBM and Xerox, who are risking reorganizational perturbations to flatten and speed their organizations, and open themselves to more continuous innovation.

Hard times also call into question more self-indulgent goals such as quality of work life and minimizing environmental degradation. What good are business ethics in a business that may be forced to close its doors and send all its people out on the street? The hard lesson we are learning is that ethics is not a luxury. The ethics we need to save us, to make us competitive in the world market, is a deep ethical wisdom. Free enterprise will encounter the age of limits and in doing so will discipline itself. The advantage to the ethical will only grow.

To flourish, we need extraordinary commitment from all employees, often to do the impossible: to achieve unprecedented quality and responsiveness in products and services along with heroic frugality, to create incredible levels of integration and collaboration, and especially to pull off continuous, brilliant, and cheap innovation. How can we begin to function at these levels?

This is where old-fashioned values are having renewed following. First, it is people who make a difference—all the people. We have relearned over the last decade simple truths without hubris: there is no way we can "manage" high-level human output, but only set the conditions for everyone doing their best: including support of the core competencies of people, their ability to self-organize, their ability to change and grow.

We are discovering that we only bring our best selves to the party when each individual is valued and free to act. Freedom only works when it is exercised with a state of mind well beyond the limits of individualism. Human self-organizing systems depend on the units within the system to behave ethically, even when they are not watched, even when there are no penalties for misbehavior. For higher levels of interconnection to manifest, there must be trust, and that trust must be based on an assurance of the goodness of others in the system.

Seven Basics

We must build cultures in which freedom and personal initiative can cohabit with cooperation, caring, and a highly integrated harmony. Effective societies and companies alike have their grounding in ethical basics that rest on freedom and democracy: the value of diversity; distributed power; continuous reality testing; distributed leadership; global ethics; acting for the long run; and the golden rule.

1. The value of diversity. A collective freedom must encompass and nourish diversity. This is what collectivism forgot—the freedom to be diverse, and the conception of each diverse individual being inherently of equal value and having open-ended potential for contribution.

The challenge of valuing diversity only begins with equal opportunity as defined by law. Within each ethnic and cultural group, there is enormous diversity that individuals bring to the workplace—diverse styles, talents, and competencies. The freedom to be diverse without being devalued is at the yeast of democracy's effectiveness. Diversity is driving the successes of flexible cross-functional teams. Further appropriate diversity is gained when teams form anew for each new project.

2. Distributed power. To have a flexible and responsive organization, intelligence must be distributed—every person using their brain, and interacting to create knowledge that is rapidly disseminated and used. Effective organizations are raising the distribution of power to an ethical principle, backed up with some level of control or ownership of assets.

The best organizations encourage new cross-functional working alliances to serve customers—and assist the dismantling and reemergence of new groupings, processes, and structures as new needs emerge. These new alliances are developing across all traditional boundaries, substituting for hierarchical simplicity an amorphous and fluctuating complexity of relationships.

Simple rules and rigid policies are not enough to guide increasingly empowered employees. There must be a shared sense of where the organization is trying to go, and then, because ends never justify means, a deep respect for ethics. The power of leadership is in providing ethical and effective power to the people.

3. Continuous reality testing. To give people freedom and power, we need continuous and principled reality testing, fully distributed. We need what Max De Pree calls "lavish communications," which only occur in cultures that promote truth and never suppress or limit the distribution of information. Organizations energized with self-organizing groups and projects that are flexible and responsive gain needed coordination—not from the power of people over people, but from continuous self-testing against broad principles and shared vision.

4. Distributed leadership. Leadership must be as distributed as intelligence—free people cannot collaborate without sharing the big picture, cannot move forward effectively without common mission, cannot self-test and self-renew without accurate feedback, cannot count on each other without trust in a common and widespread moral wisdom. Distributed leadership integrates the paradoxes inherent in human association. New organizational designs encourage equal measures of freedom and cooperation, equal doses of market discipline and community collaboration. Anyone ignoring one side of this paradox will in the end be burned by it, and so we must develop both the analytic and the heartfelt, the canny trader and the caring compatriot, the entrepreneur and the communitarian, the individualist and the egalitarian, the competitor and the partner.

5. Global ethics. Freedom extended to people embedded in a deep sense of community is the basic lesson the Japanese are teaching the world, and to hold our own we must attain the next stage of ethics beyond them—beyond a parochial definition of what the individual is part of. If the Japanese are learning to be ethical to the boundaries of Japan, we must learn to be ethical not only to the level of company and beyond to the level of our national communities, but to extend our ethical boundaries to include the world.

6. Acting for the long run. The most difficult and important technological challenge of our times is to find ways to bring the whole population up to an advanced standard of living without destroying our environment. This cannot be done with existing technology; nor will the world wait for economic progress. Good industrial ecology is already yielding savings for companies. "Pollution prevention" programs are preparing firms for the inevitable regulations and taxes to come.

7. The golden rule. "Do unto others as you would have others do unto you" is the basic rule for community survival. Those groups which survive well will treat each other and even their customers as equals, with consideration and respect. Internally, the golden rule is needed to prevent our worst behaviors—destructive in-fighting, stifling authoritarianism, diverting status-seeking. This principle is the basis of pulling together and getting anything done of value. Reality is harsh, and seems to be getting harsher. We function best when we can count on others, and others on us, and when we are willing to collaborate with our colleagues and customers on mutual goals. Every workplace that has long-term success rests on community values: mutual support, caring for each other, our customers, and the worlds we share, and being responsible to learn and change so as to produce unquestionable positive value—or jeopardize everyone's survival.

Conclusion

In some sense, everyone knows that more ethical and far-sighted behavior is necessary. Many of our problems today are the result of moral lapses, selfish excesses, and short-sightedness. In the rapids ahead, no inner guidance system will be strong and aware enough to guide empowered employees—save an unshakable desire to discover what is truly ethical and do it. This does not mean that we do not have controls or systems for encouraging the good and limiting the bad. It does mean we need to recover the old-fashioned wisdom that one of the primary jobs of leadership is to develop ethical awareness in people while bringing out their creativity and competency. It does require each of us to begin cultivating our ethical competence with the same enthusiasm we devote to cultivating our technical, marketing, and finance skills.

Business organizations have contributed to the problems of the world—we can point to pollution, materialism, and alienation. Yet modern corporations have within them the powers of change. Those companies that seize the ethical initiative will define the future and be around to enjoy it.

Gifford and Elizabeth Pinchot, chairman and president of Pinchot & Co., are contributing editors to Executive Excellence. *They are the authors of* The End of Bureaucracy and the Rise of the Intelligent Organization.

Chapter 11

New Bottom Lines

**By Frank K. Sonnenberg and
Beverly Goldberg**

We need to formulate our own personal bottom lines, keeping in mind that self and society are not mutually exclusive.

In the not-so-distant past, one's word was sacrosanct; friendship meant being available in bad times as well as good; doctor-patient relationships implied caring and respect; and partnerships had meaning beyond legal papers. In those days, relationships between suppliers and customers went beyond price; parenting meant more than meeting physical needs; bankers were pillars of the community; and being a citizen meant accepting certain civic obligations.

Today, our society is turning into a world with amnesia: Everything important seems to have been forgotten. *Trust, honor,* and *loyalty* are words that have little meaning today. Doctors check credit references before treating the ill; publishers value commercialism over literary excellence; holidays are about shopping and parties, not about family and religion; policemen, athletes, and teachers—once role models for our children—are now accused of savagely beating citizens, betting on sporting events, and altering student test scores to promote their own reputations. Politicians touted as senatorial or presidential material drop out of contention for high office because of scandals, and one out of two marriages ends in divorce.

And according to one survey, "Two in every three people today believe that there is nothing wrong with telling a lie. Only 31 percent of us believe that honesty is the best policy." The new ethic seems to be: "If it's not convenient, I won't make the effort; if it's not beneficial right now, I'm not interested; and if it's not as advantageous to me today as when I made the promise, I won't honor my commitments."

Look at the ease with which relationships are ended, partnerships dissolved, and laws broken, and think about how business deals once made on the basis of a handshake now require thick contracts—and still end in litigation. The laws, moral codes, religious principles, and ethical standards that once governed our behavior no longer seem to have a place in our society. The rules—written and unwritten—that once made social and business life simple have been violated so often that those who follow them are often regarded with contempt.

The costs of this trend to business are enormous. How many of your employees isolate themselves because they've been burned by betrayals of confidence? How many managers spend hours checking up on subordinates who have not lived up to promises made in the past? How many people spend all their time "covering their behinds," "putting it in writing," or "reading the small print," rather than getting their work done? These actions encourage cynicism among employees and a belief that the impression they make is more important than the work they produce.

The costs to our society are just as grave. How many couples fail to build relationships with their spouses because they don't trust the marriage will last? How many people decide not to vote because they don't believe candidates keep campaign pledges? And how many people refuse to give donations to charity because they think the money goes to those who run the organizations instead of those in need? When 50 percent of those eligible to vote don't, when 30 percent of spouses cheat, when the *Harvard Business Review* runs an article pointing out that honesty doesn't necessarily bring economic rewards, the time has come to think about where we are going.

Can You Sleep at Night?

All too many people lose sleep because of an unfocused anxiety. They are worried about the future. They don't know if they can believe that this is the last round of layoffs, whether the supplier who promised delivery next week will come through, or if the line will be held on taxes. We no longer trust people to tell us the truth, to do what is right rather than what is politically expedient, to live up to their commitments—or to care about adhering to a code of honor. In a labor-intensive society, hard work resulted in tired bones and muscles. In the information age, our bodies react with stress-related ailments ranging from headaches to backaches to anxiety attacks.

We have no time for things that are important. We judge someone's worth by what we see on the outside. We envy people who achieve success without thinking about what they did to earn it.

If we seek instant gratification, view customers as transactions rather than lifelong relationships, and see employees as instruments to increase the bottom line rather than partners in our business, then we shouldn't be surprised when we get what we deserve, or wonder why our business has stopped growing.

We tend to work at such a frenetic pace that we want everything said in three bullet points to save time. We stop at the very first answer that we find rather than seeking the best solution. We focus on the sizzle rather than on the content. As a result, subtlety and nuance are lost, and everyone assumes that we have no time for content. No wonder the media, with its focus on ratings, present afternoon talk shows featuring oddities rather than new developments. No wonder our children think of the abnormal as normal and the unacceptable as the norm rather than an exception to the rule.

In the past, parenting meant providing quality time, not trying to buy our children's love. Today, we leave parenting to schools and television. We don't take the time to instill morals and values, to listen, to play with our children when we are at home. Instead, our focus is on the job, on accumulating possessions, on trying to live up to expectations.

Where are our heroes—people we can admire not only for their achievements but also for their noble qualities? If we want our children to admire those who combine native talent with noble qualities, we need to convey our definitions of a hero to them, and live by the words that we speak. For example, your gift to a charity is doubled when you tell your children why you are donating it and convey to them the need to give.

Do Good People Finish Last?

All too many people believe that there is no correlation between integrity and bottom-line performance. They are wrong. Integrity and performance are not polar opposites. When people work for an organization that they believe is fair, they are willing to give of themselves to get the job done; traditions of loyalty and caring are hallmarks; and people work to a higher standard. The values around them become part of them, and they think of the customer as someone to whom they owe the finest possible product and service.

Because they believe in the mission of their organization, they no longer distinguish between their own reputation and the reputation of their organization. They work harder to live up to the promise of their word, to exceed customer expectations, to ensure that products are flawless, and to produce on time and within budget. In other words, they take pride in their work. When that happens, an organization builds a reputation for quality, and that reputation draws more customers, increasing market share.

This is a very different environment than one in which a job is just a job. You notice the difference when you walk down the halls. You can quickly tell how things are going without reading the financials. People enjoy what they are doing. They know the guy down the hall isn't after their job because he's too busy doing his own. Compensation is more than a weekly paycheck—it includes the care expressed for people through efforts to let them know that they are needed and that they are making a real contribution.

Those who believe that people are motivated only by money, that people are too selfish to respond to a worthy cause, are not looking around them. How many people come home tired from work but find energy to make telephone calls and attend meetings for charity, because they believe in the cause?

The difference in attitudes between those who work for many large organizations and those who work for entrepreneurial growth companies is similar: It is the difference between doing a job for a paycheck and doing a job because of a belief in what you are doing. The passion, the excitement, the desire to win at all costs, the never-give-up attitude, are the result of buying into a vision and into what the organization represents. No matter what side people are on, their belief in a cause, in doing the right thing, drives them.

Without psychic rewards, no amount of money will ever feel like enough. In addition to a fair salary, people are paid by feeling good about what they do. They want to work where they can establish friendships; where they can take pride in what they contribute and in what the organization stands for. People want to know that when their company's product is sold, they can honestly tell their customers, "You will be happy, because you've just bought the best."

New Bottom Lines

In business, the new bottom lines mean you don't jump down someone's throat when they make a mistake; you make it clear you know they're trying to do their best—and they will respond in kind. It also means that you don't just hire bodies: you seek valued employees to join to your business family. You invest in your people. You are not out to sell your customers, but to service them now and in the future. Your responsibilities go beyond the next quarter's financials to build a legacy for those who follow.

Being true to ourselves does not mean harming or ignoring others; honesty has to be more than obeying the letter of the law. Being loyal to others means assuming that they will keep their word and letting them know that we will keep ours.

Contracts may be needed to formalize an arrangement, but they should not substitute for honorable relationships. We lose something tangible when we abandon such intangibles as loyalty, honor, and trust.

Frank K. Sonnenberg is president of RMI Marketing and Advertising and the author of Marketing to Win. *Beverly Goldberg is vice-president, The Twentieth Century Fund, a New York-based think tank, and principal of Siberg Consulting.*

What Is Ethical Judgment?

Chapter 12

Ethical Judgment

By Sherry Baker

We can stimulate and sharpen moral reasoning and ethical judgment by considering decisions in light of certain questions.

Ethics in the workplace (applied ethics) has become a hot topic in recent years. Business book titles and academic textbooks and journals are now replete with volumes on ethics.

Why all the concern? We live in a world where new technologies and communication systems have given rise to new ethical questions; where concern for profits often come into conflict with concern for principles; where professions and specializations recognize a need to identify and encourage professional values; and where society is demanding an ethic of social responsibility for corporate action.

Also, there is disturbing evidence of patently unethical behavior all around us—from employee theft of time and materials, to corporate social and environmental irresponsibility, to the unethical and illegal activities of our political and religious leaders. Professionals and scholars have responded with professional codes of ethics, articles about ethics, and courses in ethics, all resulting in more discourse about ethical issues and a greater availability of ethics-related material.

Moral Dilemmas

Despite all this new discourse, executives who face troubling decisions are often confused about how to arrive at the right, the moral, the ethical course of action. This is not surprising since by definition a "moral dilemma" is one where there is no clear right and wrong, only positives and negatives.

Tip-of-the-tongue guidelines such as "Love thy neighbor" rarely suffice when one is faced with an ethical dilemma where no course of action seems to satisfy all ethical responsibilities.

Writers disagree about how to reach an ethical decision or about what criteria must be met for a course of action to be ethical. Some ethicists, for example, stress the need to be concerned with ethical outcomes or consequences, while others are interested in basing action on ethical principles regardless of the outcome; some stress the importance of developing a sterling character, while others focus on issues of justice.

While it may be problematic to come up with a set of principles that apply in all cases, I do not to espouse moral relativity. Some actions are clearly more ethical than others. We can be guided in our moral reasoning by the insight that comes from asking ourselves tough questions about personal principles, codes of conduct, the moral rights of others, justice, consequences, outcomes, decisions, intuition, and insight. I include *intuition* because our judgments often must be rough and intuitive and made, as Manuel G. Velasquez says, at "the edges of the light that ethics can shed on moral reasoning."

Questions to Ask

Assuming a difficult decision, consider how the following questions might help in identifying points of ethical concern.

Principles and Codes of Conduct

• Does this decision or action meet up to my standards about how people should interact with each other?

•Does this decision or action agree with my religious teachings and beliefs (or my personal principles and sense of responsibility)?

• How will I feel about myself if I do this?

• Do we (or I) have a rule or policy for cases like this?

• Would I want everyone to make the same decision and take the same action if faced with these same circumstances?

• What are my true motives for considering this action?

Moral Rights

• Would this action infringe or impinge on the moral rights or dignity of others?

• Would this action allow others freedom of choice in this matter?

• Would this action involve deceiving others in any way?

Justice

• Would I feel that this action was just (ethical or fair) if I were on the other side of the decision?

• How would I feel if this action were done to me or to someone close to me?

• Would this action or decision distribute benefits justly?

• Would it distribute hardships or burdens justly?

• Would this action infringe on the moral rights of others?

Consequences and Outcomes

• What will be the short- and long-term consequences?

- Who will benefit from this course of action?
- Who will be hurt?
- How will this action create good and prevent harm?

Public Explanation or Defense of Decisions
- How will I feel when this action becomes public knowledge?
- Can I explain adequately to others why I took this action?
- Would others feel that my action or decision is ethical? right? moral?

Intuition and Insight
- Have I searched for all alternatives? Are there other ways I could look at this situation? Have I considered all points of view?

- Even if there is sound rationality for this decision or action, and even if I could defend it publicly, do I believe this is right?

- What does my intuition tell me is the ethical thing to do in this situation? Have I listened to my inner voice?

Moral Reasoning

These questions could be helpful for decision making and for fruitful group discussions when considered in light of specific cases or hypothetical scenarios. Examples of actual difficult cases to discuss can be found in a company's own experience, in newspapers or periodicals, or in business ethics books.

We can stretch and expand our moral reasoning and ethical judgment, and sharpen our ethical sensitivity and moral awareness by thinking through dilemmas in light of these questions.

Often what appears to be an ethical decision in light of one consideration might appear to be less ethical in light of another. Eventually we must weigh all alternatives and decide which criteria deserve the highest priority in the particular circumstance facing us.

Identifying the points of difficulty with clarity allows us to decide what values or considerations must have the most weight in our deliberations and decisions. We are then better prepared to make a decision that is both right and defensible.

Ethical dilemmas are poignant in ways that other dilemmas are not because they are concerned with the positive or negative impact of people's actions on other people; with issues of right and wrong, good and bad. We must always weigh our obligation to prevent and alleviate harm. The answers are never easy or absolute, and well-meaning people can disagree on a proper course of action. Still, when faced with an ethical dilemma, we can be confident that if we consider all questions with real intent and pure motives, our moral reasoning and insight will lead us to sound and ethical decisions.

Sherry Baker, Ph.D., is Assistant Academic Dean at LDS Business College in Salt Lake City, Utah.

Chapter 13

Celestial Navigation

By Charles Bennett

For many years sailors have relied on the stars to navigate their way across the great oceans of earth. Stars are fantastic navigational aids because they remain from our perspective in steady, predictable places in the heavens. To determine their position, sailors would gaze into the sky at night and "shoot" the visible stars with a sextant. From this information, they could locate themselves on what Carl Sagan has called our "pale blue dot." This method of navigation is called celestial navigation. Today sailors primarily use electronic navigational systems, but many are still trained to navigate by the stars should these modern satellite and land-based positioning systems fail.

Celestial navigation provides an excellent metaphor for thinking about the role of values and ethical standards in organizational life. While changes in the world are happening at a fast and furious pace, people's ideal, desired states of existence (their values) and their criteria for determining good from bad, right from wrong (their ethical standards) provide stable navigational aids for steering a proactive, principled, and consistent course. In short, they are the primary factors motivating and guiding our choices, ostensibly leading us towards a "better" life and world. Values, and especially ethical standards, are the stars that remain in the sky as reliable, steady navigational aids no matter how rough the seas and turbulent the winds become. Without these stars, our direction is dictated almost completely by external forces such as the sea state and wind conditions—representing such things as socialization, competition, peer pressure, conflict, or simply unexpected changes.

While technological aids have given us the ability to navigate on the globe with amazing efficiency, we still need to regularly calibrate these instruments in relation to the stars to ensure that they provide us with accurate information. They also are dependent upon the larger celestial system of which the earth is one small part. What happens when we don't calibrate our modern systems on a regular basis? What happens when we stare at them day and night as though they themselves had within them the order of the heavens? We would slowly but surely drift off course, and head in a direction unknown to us—all the while believing we were on track. This happens to many organizations, particularly in times of rapid change.

Almost all executives now rely on some sort of technologies to guide them efficiently through problem solving, decision making, and the production and distribution of their goods and services. However, our true navigational aids can only be identified, clarified, and understood through an open, thorough examination of our values and ethical standards and of the systems we have created in their image. Technology, despite our determined efforts, cannot substitute for the effort required to develop this awareness and clarity of thought.

So what happens when we become obsessed with our modern, technological systems and avoid the effort necessary to understand our stars (i.e., our values and ethical ideals)? At this point, we essentially know only the look of high tech information sources. In the process, we virtually forget how to make sense of ourselves as living, breathing, growing beings. In this situation, how do we determine what is "good" or "right" for us? What paths should we take, and how can we discover them?

The answers to these questions emerge at the other end of self-reflection focused on the clarification of our values and ethical standards and how they relate to every choice that we make. The results of this examination lead us to an understanding and internalization of simple, yet profound and timeless principles—like the stars that are the basis for celestial navigation.

If individuals and organizations are successfully to steer their way through these seas, they must never lose sight of the values and ethical standards that are the ultimate referents in their celestial navigation system. How does an organization engage in the identification and clarification of these principles? Based on a review of the literature, and on my own experiences in introducing people to these concepts and facilitating their search for ethical clarity, I offer four suggestions.

• *This process takes time and effort,* regardless of whether it is undertaken in the context of problem solving, decision making, strategic planning, or developing a mission statement. Because this process forces many people for the first time to deal with relatively complex issues such as their own and others' values and ethics, a canned, time-saving "program" to identify a core set of values, talk about them a bit, and draft a values statement will fail to clarify the guiding principles that lie at the heart of an organization's culture. In short, this is not a quick-fix endeavor. It will not eliminate the conflicts and tensions inherent in organizational life. It will, however, help you deal with conflicts more effectively as they arise.

• *Senior management must have the courage to risk discovering hidden assumptions and standards,* make these explicit, and allow them to be topics for open, respectful dialogue involving the entire organization. Top-down, blue-ribbon committee approaches will not result in the internalization of a selected set of values and ethical standards. It will, on the other hand, probably result in a round of cynicism that saps employee motivation, focus, and dedication. Senior management must be willing to align systems with the values and ethical standards that are to be guiding principles. Management must be willing to lead the organization "across the Rubicon." If they fail to "walk their talk" after starting this process, the problems associated with hypocrisy and inconsistency will be far more noticeable and difficult to deal with.

• *The specific steps that people take in gaining clarity about their values and ethical standards will inevitably differ from one organization to the next.* Because much of this work entails personal discovery that is synergistically transferred to the organization as a whole, attempts to apply one-size-fits-all approaches will stifle progress. A constant balancing act between providing structure, focus, and direction and allowing the organization to find its own way through uncertainty, confusion, and discovery must be struck by facilitators of this reflective process.

• *The dialogue and reflection at the heart of this process should continually be linked to real experiences and, most importantly, to actual results being sought.* This will minimize the chance that participants will feel they are engaged in some abstract exercise that has little if any application to the "real world." By constantly grounding the content of the dialogue to real experiences, problems, decisions, and objectives, more interest in the process will be generated, the chances for shared learning and buy-in will be increased, and the ability to implement the lessons learned will be enhanced.

Organizations that accept the challenge to identify and clarify their navigational stars will be far more able to sustain their strategic leadership, competitive advantage, and profitability as we continue to experience the profound economic, social, environmental, cultural, and political changes ushering in the 21st century.

For those of you who take the time and effort to undertake such a process, I wish you the traditional sailors' blessing—"Fair winds, following seas, and Godspeed."

Charles Bennett, Ph.D., is the Director of Research at the California Center for Civic Renewal, Santa Barbara, California.

Chapter 14

Moral Compassing

By Stephen R. Covey

When managing in the wilderness of the changing times, a map is of limited worth. What's needed is a moral compass.

Once when I was in New York City, I witnessed a mugging skillfully executed by a street gang. I'm sure that the members of this gang have their street maps, their common values—the highest value being, be true and loyal to each other—but this value, as it's interpreted and practiced by this gang, does not represent "true north"—the magnetic principle of respect for people and property.

They lacked an internal moral compass. Principles are like a compass. A compass has a *true north* that is objective and external, that reflects natural laws or principles, as opposed to values which are subjective and internal. Because the compass represents the eternal verities of life, we must develop our value system with deep respect for "true north" principles.

As Cecil B. deMille said about the principles in his movie, *The Ten Commandments:* "It is impossible for us to break the law. We can only break ourselves against the law."

Principles are proven, enduring guidelines for human conduct. Certain principles govern human effectiveness. The six major world religions all teach the same basic core beliefs—such principles as "you reap what you sow" and "actions are more important than words." I find global consensus around what "true north" principles are. These are not difficult to detect. They are objective, basic, unarguable: "You can't have trust without being trustworthy" and "You can't talk yourself out of a problem you behave yourself into."

There is little disagreement in what the constitutional principles of a company should be when enough people get together. I find a universal belief in: fairness, kindness, dignity, charity, integrity, honesty, quality, service, patience.

Consider the absurdity of trying to live a life or run a business based on the opposites. I doubt that anyone would seriously consider unfairness, deceit, baseness, uselessness, mediocrity, or degradation to be a solid foundation for lasting happiness and success.

People may argue about how these principles are to be defined, interpreted, and applied in real-life situations, but they generally agree about their intrinsic merit. They may not live in total harmony with them, but they believe in them. And, they want to be managed by them. They want to be evaluated by "laws" in the social and economic dimensions that are just as real, just as unchanging and unarguable, as laws such as gravity are in the physical dimension.

In any serious study of history—be it national or corporate—the reality and verity of such principles become obvious. These principles surface time and again, and the degree to which people in a society recognize and live in harmony with them moves them toward either survival and stability or disintegration and destruction.

In a talk show interview, I was once asked if Hitler was principle-centered. "No," I said, "but he was value-driven. One of his governing values was to unify Germany. But he violated compass principles and suffered the natural consequences. And the consequences were momentous—the dislocation of the entire world for years."

In dealing with self-evident, natural laws, we can choose either to manage in harmony with them or to challenge them. Just as the laws are fixed, so too are the consequences. In my seminars, I ask audiences, "When you think of your personal values, how do you think?" Typically, people focus on what they want. I then ask them, "When you think of principles, how do you think?" They are more oriented toward objective law, listening to conscience, tapping into eternal verities.

Principles are not values. The German Nazis, like the street gang members, shared values, but these violated basic principles. Values are maps. Principles are territories. And the maps are not the territories; they are only subjective attempts to describe or represent the territory.

The more closely our maps are aligned with correct principles— with the realities of the territory, with things as they are—the more accurate and useful they will be. Correct maps will impact our effectiveness far more than our efforts to change attitudes and behaviors.

However, when the territory is constantly changing, when the markets are constantly shifting, any map is soon obsolete.

A Compass for the Times

In today's world, what's needed is a compass. A compass consists of a magnetic needle swinging freely and pointing to magnetic north. It's also a mariner's instrument for directing or ascertaining the course of ships at sea as well as an instrument for drawing circles and taking measurements. The word *compass* may also refer to the reach, extent, limit or boundary of a space or time; a course, circuit or range; an intent, purpose or design; an understanding or comprehension. All of these connotations enrich the meaning of the metaphor.

Why is a compass better than a map in today's world? I see several compelling reasons why the compass is so invaluable.

- The compass orients people to the coordinates and indicates a course or direction even in forests, deserts, seas, and open terrain.

- As the territory changes, the map becomes obsolete; in times of change, a map may be dated and inaccurate by the time it's printed.

- Inaccurate maps are sources of great frustration for people who are trying to find their way or navigate territory.

- Many executives are pioneering, managing in uncharted waters or wilderness, and no existing map accurately describes the territory.

- To get anywhere very fast, we need refined processes and clear channels of production and distribution (freeways), and to find or create freeways in the wilderness, we need a compass.

- The map provides description, but the compass provides more vision and direction.

- An accurate map is a good management tool, but a compass is a leadership and an empowerment tool.

People who have used maps for many years to find their way and maintain a sense of perspective and direction should realize that their maps may be useless in the current maze of management. My recommendation is that you exchange your map for a compass and train yourself and your people how to navigate by a compass calibrated to a set of fixed, true north principles and natural laws.

Strategic Orientation

Map-versus-compass orientation is an important strategic issue. The old strategic planning model is obsolete. It locked us into certain mindsets or paradigms, into management by maps, into an old model of leadership where the experts at the top decide the objectives, methods, and means.

The old model is like a road map. It calls for people at the top to exercise their experience, expertise, wisdom and judgment and set 10-year strategic plans—only to find that the plans are worthless within 18 months. In the new environment, plans become obsolete fast. As Peter Drucker noted: "Plans are worthless, but planning is invaluable."

If our planning is centered on an overall purpose or vision and on a commitment to set of principles, then the people who are closest to the action in the wilderness can use that compass and their own expertise and judgment to make decisions and take actions. In effect, each person may have his or her own compass; each may be empowered to make plans that reflect the realities of the new market.

Principles are not practices. Practices are specific activities or actions that work in one circumstance but not necessarily in another. If you manage by practices and lead by policies, your people don't have to be the experts; they don't have to exercise judgment, because all judgment and wisdom are provided in the form of rules.

If you focus on principles, you empower everyone who understands those principles to act without constant monitoring, evaluating, correcting, or controlling. Principles have universal application. And when these are internalized into habits, they empower people to create a wide variety of practices to deal with different situations.

Leading by principles, as opposed to practices, requires a different training, perhaps even more training, but the payoff is more expertise, creativity, and shared responsibility at all levels.

If you train people in the practices of customer service, you will get a degree of customer service, but the service will break down whenever customers present a special case or problem. Before people will consistently act on the principle of customer service, they need to adopt a new mindset. In most cases, they need to be trained—using cases, role plays, simulations and coaching—to understand how the principle is applied on the job.

With the Compass, We Can Win

"A compass in every pocket" is better than "a chicken in very pot" or a car in every garage.

But once people start to realize that this "compass" is going to be the basis for evaluation, including the leadership style of the people at the top, they tend to feel very threatened.

The idea of moral compassing is unsettling to people who think they are above the law. Because the constitution, based on principles, is the law—it governs everybody, including the president. It places responsibility on individuals to examine their lives and determine if they are willing to live by the constitution.

Michael Porter has said: "An implementation with B strategy is better than A strategy with B implementation." We must deal with issues to improve the implementation of strategy and to achieve corporate integrity. We must be willing to go through a constitutional convention, if not a revolutionary war, to get the issues out on the table, deal with them, and get deep buy-in on the decisions. That won't happen without some blood, sweat, and tears.

Ultimately, the successful implementation of any strategy hinges on the integrity people have to the governing principles and on their ability to apply those principles in any situation using their own moral compass.

Stephen R. Covey is co-chairman of the FranklinCovey Company.

Chapter 15

The Quest for Corporate Values

By Allan Cox

Values are many things to many people. Values are sometimes described as having either a lot or a little to do with morals or ethics. They are also spoken of as priority rating systems.

I find it ironic that value systems often seem impulsively-developed, whether viewed as benchmarks for tolerance of the thoughts and behavior of others or our own willingness to cope with inconveniences to reach goals or cultivate respected character traits.

These strongly-defended character components are often vulnerable to circumstances. At numerous points in our lives, they tend to change with the wind. Negative as this will-o-the-wisp movement may sound, such malleability may be beneficial.

Our values often change as our institutions change. The fact that we accept such change indicates that some new priority is given sanction by some institution in which we have invested authority and trust. In effect, we willingly trade some of our old values for new institutionally approved ones in order to participate in the institution's objectives and benefits.

Although frequently criticized for depersonalization or indifference to personal goals, values and objectives, the corporation provides the best example of the positive institutionalization of personal value systems. The corporate enterprise is successful overall because it interweaves the values of its employees with its own to achieve its goals. For most of us, the corporation provides the first startling value alteration experience of our adult lives. In corporate environments, we are seriously encouraged to shed our more self-serving values in exchange for team values and group objectives. We are asked to work within a group rather than primarily as individuals.

Degrees of personal individuality are tolerated, indeed welcomed, but the common experience is one where newcomers shift their focus from individual values to group values.

They who adapt to these new, team-oriented values will be more at ease and effective. They and the corporation will hold the same objectives in common. They who find their individuality difficult to part with also will find life within the corporate community difficult to adapt to and to grow in, and ultimately they will be rejected by that community. New members who fail to adopt the prevailing values are likely to fail in contributing to its daily functions.

Without values and codes that direct expectations, individuals and groups alike will roam aimlessly, greatly limited in meeting and satisfying their longed-for levels of achievement.

We can compare values to cellular components of the body's arterial network. They provide directions that steer us to our goals. Like the body's arterial courseway, when any aspect of the value structure is disrupted or functions poorly, the entire system suffers, sometimes fatally. Value disorientation is a major symptom of most life crises. By adapting quickly and by replacing outmoded principles, or returning to needed but "lost" ones, we enhance our ability to meet our goals and expectations.

Values and Morals

Values and morals are not the same. Morals are universally developed systems of thought and practice that tend more to guarantee group survival and welfare than serve as individual guidance in establishing and reaching personal goals. For example, amoral and immoral persons can and do possess complex value systems. Hitler imparted his values throughout his country, resulting in the extermination of 6,000,000 Jews. We all know that he was not a moral man. But who would deny the great value he placed on power?

Values are guiding devices to enhance our ability to achieve our purposes. Objectively, values have limited direct relation to right and wrong. They outline desirable alternatives, less desirable alternatives, and unthinkable alternatives within our daily decision-making. As we become the owner of a specific system of values, every choice we make and action we take is affected by the nature of that system.

Most people tend to pride themselves on their values. Presumably, all we do and say reflects our internalized collective values. Yet there is a large element of self-orientation to the development of such systems. Our values say much about how we see ourselves. They convey what we cherish and prize in life. Commonly, we relate our values with pride and enthusiasm to win appreciation from others.

Loyalties to family, nation, religion, political parties and sometimes even sports teams tend to be passed within families from one generation to the next. In youth, we are usually eager to go along with these values. We seek acceptance and approval from peers and relevant authorities, so we value the things we are taught to value.

In adult life, we assess our values more critically, discarding some bequeathed values of youth and acquiring new values that reflect our own goals more directly. We select groups to join that share our values.

Corporate managers seek out professional groups that aid in the development of their career and skills on their jobs. Professional associations provide continuing education and the chance to network with others who share similar values and management beliefs.

The group reciprocates by assisting individuals who support it. It shares their values and helps them win their fellow member's financial, emotional, and voluntary backing. Without such backing, the group cannot exist or effectively live up to its charter. The mutual benefit to group and member alike, then, is dependent on mutual exchange and gratification of individuals and the group as a whole. Satisfying priority values of individuals members is the cornerstone to group survival.

So complex are some group values that they are hard to define, sometimes difficult to observe. But they are as deeply rooted as individual values. Groups cannot exist without goals; goals cannot be met without action; action cannot be taken without choices; choices cannot be made without falling back on values.

Top executives who can identify the prevailing values of their corporations mark themselves, hands-down, as most able to lead it.

Changing Values

Contrary to popular belief, changing values and goals are often symptomatic of growth rather than lack of direction or poor planning. There is significant difference between the man who is in and out of several careers by the time he is 35 and the one, age 45, who, after achieving most career objectives, decides to try his hand at something new.

With our publicized, advertised, touted accent on individuality and self-fulfillment, mid-life traumas are most common. At such times, some people not only question long-held values, but cast a gimlet eye on their gains and worth of their achievements. What we expect ourselves to achieve usually grows out of a vital seed planted and well-nurtured early in life.

Articles, documentaries, dramas, and various other sorts of media about self-fulfillment often tempt us to alter our values and re-evaluate our lives. According to a survey by Daniel Yankelovich and described in his book, *New Rules,* this search for self-fulfillment was the consuming one of 80 percent of Americans during the last two decades. We have now entered a period of new commitment.

Once people's lives were rarely upset by the quiet comings and goings of life changes. Today, these cycles often bring crisis, turmoil, and upheaval likely to alter the individual's entire life. Divorces, career changes, and major moves are often events that take place in an atmosphere resulting from drastic value change.

Value changes in themselves need not alter lifestyles. Newly considered values of freedom are sometimes rejected in favor of older, more traditional values of security and comfort. Ironically, sometimes these "new" values turn out to be the oldest values, those we had buried in all the climbing and striving, that re-emerge—seemingly new, but not—in the service of that "life-goal" we have been only "dimly aware of."

Values in Conflict

At their smallest, conflicts in values for individuals consist of irrationalities or inconsistencies. Scattered among crucial points in our lives, we make choices. If we're fortunate, we do this with a minimum of pain. Other times, we make decisions unwittingly, unaware of our selection of values.

We sometimes find ourselves at a crossroad and able to choose our course only after painful deliberation. Painful as they may be, they come to pass. And we live with the decisions we make during such times, occasionally with regret.

On the other hand, groups sometimes never quite recover from a bad decision in response to value conflicts. The good news is that in most cases, common goals within our institutions act as a gyroscope to override the conflict of the day.

The Corporate Culture

If culture consists of the "man-made aspects of the organizational environment," then it is obvious that the values of the corporation are an integral part of its culture; and they are adopted to serve the corporation's goals.

Consultants and executives proudly espouse "management-by-values" or "value-based management." This is a bit silly since all corporations manage themselves based on values. The issue is, are the values by which they are managed "good" ones? That is, do they serve the wider good of all society? Most do.

At the corporate level, ability to spread common values to those inducted into the ranks, ability to make favorable decisions in the face of changing values, ability to overcome conflicting values between and among members are essential to success and growth. The corporation—with its success or failure, with its numerous daily decisions, with its tendency to grow or to decay—affects the lives of us all.

To some critics, corporations represent all that is wrong with capitalism. The criticism they point at the corporation includes depersonalization, corruption, and a host of other charges of inhumanity and fraud.

Still, it is within the corporation that our social ideals of democracy are most realized. Reflecting on that paradox of capitalism, Lewis Lapham once suggested, "If a price can be set on the worth of a man's labor but not on his dreams or his hope of the future, then the mainspring of capitalism must rest on a paradox. In the realm of politics, the paradox presents itself between the pressure for social justice and the inertia of greed."

As we shift from dominance of greed to social justice and back again, we manage to stay on our feet while achieving profit, creativity, and survival. Nowhere is this better exemplified than at the corporate level. Successful merging of corporate values with individual values is the basis for a successful enterprise.

Most vital to the organization's success is the relationship between the corporation and its managers. The crux of this relationship lies in how corporations perceive their managers, what they expect from them in terms of lifestyle and workstyle, and how managers perceive their organizations.

While there are many differences in background and qualifications among managers of any given corporation, there exists one common—though hard to capture—denominator. And the essence of that denominator concerns the individual's ability to sense, translate, and communicate the corporation's value system to staff, labor forces, and the corporation's various publics.

Successful executives seem to have an instinct for the values within the business. Henry Ford II is a good example. He took over his family's ailing business with some of the poorest credentials a person could have. Having flunked out of Yale twice, specializing in nothing in particular, at the time he was forced to take charge of his father's company, the only redeeming characteristic he possessed was enough to save the company. "He has gasoline in his blood," someone said of him, and it was that component that enabled him to see the business out of the pit.

Effective managers have that same sense for the business; in fact, these individuals are so possessed of that it is almost "in the blood." Effective executives are not genetically produced—they are a cultural product—but they are sometimes so inspiring or so ingenious that they become larger than life to us. Lee Iacocca, once fired by Henry Ford II, is a case in point.

Among the ranks of management can be found executives who symbolize the corporation's spirit and image. They are the clear embodiment of the corporation's values. Top executives in a corporation are individuals whose own values, for the most part, comply with and complement those of the organization.

These executives have successfully adapted to their corporation's code of values. And they have to be good at demonstrating their mastery of these values to a chief executive if they are going to succeed. Surprising to many, most top executives do not write the music. Rather, they're the conductors who learned the score in earlier years by singing in the choir; and the most enduring, effective, powerful, influential ones realize that their present task is to make sure all sections sing their parts on key.

Allan Cox heads his own Chicago-based consulting firm specializing in top management team effectiveness and executive development. He is the author of five books and serves as board chairman of The Center for Ethics and Corporate Policy.

Chapter 16

Heroic Results

By Rob Lebow

*I*magine an organization where everyone puts the interests of others first, where managers and employees freely mentor each other, where everyone is open to new ideas, truth is common, and trust abounds. A place where taking risks is encouraged and people are given credit for their accomplishments. I call those places heroic environments.

They aren't fiction. I've seen them. I've helped create them. You, too, can have one. How? By installing the operating system that melds shared values into the elements of transformation.

Recently, I talked with an old friend from Microsoft. Almost 10 years earlier, we worked together to introduce a new user-interface operating system, a concept which revolutionized software technology. The market came to know this product as Windows 2.0. After leaving Microsoft, I began searching for the "Rosetta Stone" of business. The unearthing of the Rosetta Stone was the 19th Century's greatest archeological triumph. This large tablet held the secrets to deciphering Egyptian hieroglyphics.

My challenge was to find the catalyst to meld social psychology—how people relate, behave, and act in groups—and organization development, the means whereby people can risk changing their old social norms (hidden feelings and rationalized behavior) to a more open and honest behaviors.

I believed that many businesses were faltering in trying to reinvent themselves. And all the customer service and quality initiatives in the world wouldn't save them unless they grounded their business cultures in something substantial. No single application, no silver bullet, no program or flavor of the month will fix dysfunctional areas caused by a greater problem, issue, challenge, or need; only a unifying set of elements, concepts, philosophy, instructions, or standards will do.

What is needed is a link between the company's interests and people's needs. I wanted to find a way to help organizations make profits and serve people's interests at the same time. Imagine: making money without sacrificing people.

Over the past 20 years, few organizations have harnessed the potential to improve performance and productivity. One reason is the difficulty of consistently uniting individual goals and aspirations to organizational goals. Many valiant efforts have been made in the past, most focusing on personal or individual fixes, improvements, or discoveries. In most cases, results were spotty and difficult to sustain. We would hear of excellent companies, but then hear of regressions in this success, with no constant reproducible success formula. Was there no universal approach?

My friend smiled as he listened to what I had been doing. He knew from personal experience what I meant. He understood the Rosetta Stone metaphor. He knew that I was trying to link people to the organization, just as Bill Gates, the co-founder of Microsoft, was trying to link people to the computer.

Bill knew that he had to find a way to increase access to the computer and to reinvent the way people access information. Not only did he succeed beyond his wildest dreams, but his vision ushered in a new era of technological advancements.

My challenge was to reorder the way we looked at our business problems, goals, competition, and people. I asked, "What do people want and need in their organization to be more productive and to perform at the top of their game?" Because I didn't know what my "stone" would look like, I remained open to anything. I interviewed hundreds of business people, scanned libraries, and haunted bookstores, looking for new ideas about what people needed to be productive. After all the searching, I knew that no one person or group had the full answer. In short, no one realized the power or necessity of an operating system approach.

Then one day I happened upon the Rosetta Stone by accident. It was such an unexpected and profound discovery that I didn't recognize it on sight. I found this Rosetta Stone lying dormant in a national research organization. It was an unused archival database of 17 million completed surveys from 40 countries on what people wanted at work to be happy, productive, creative, and competitive.

When I asked about purchasing the data, I was told that I could have it for free. It had been there for 25 years. Each year the baseline data was normalized, but the data was deemed worthless. I was overwhelmed. Here was my Rosetta Stone, the secret to any executive's wildest dreams for unparalleled productivity, motivation, empowerment, engagement, and focus—and it had been lying in an unmarked grave for over 25 years. When I analyzed this data, I realized that it represented fundamental human values of major proportion: 1) Treat others with uncompromising truth; 2) Lavish trust on your associates; 3) Mentor unselfishly; 4) Be receptive to new ideas, regardless of origin; 5) Take risks for the organization's sake; 6) Give credit where it's due; 7) Do not touch dishonest dollars; 8) Put the interests of others before your own.

I call these eight elements the "Shared Values of the Heroic Environment," after the late Joseph Campbell's lifelong work. Campbell defined the Heroic Act as an act of selflessness. Selfless behavior is the key to everything: It creates great friendships, working relationships, and organizations. The concept transcends culture, nationality, and time.

Over the last seven years, I've come to recognize that five modules complete the full operating system: 1) Shared values process; 2) Value-based consensus building; 3) Personal empowerment and responsibility; 4) Value-based decision making; and 5) Autonomous, self-managed, customer-centered, team-based work environment.

Shared values tie universal human needs and aspirations to organizational goals, strategies, and vision in a process that creates a dynamic balance between our business values and needs and our people values and needs.

People values are those basic human issues that affect daily work performance—values such as honesty, truthfulness, trust, risk-taking, and receptivity to new ideas. The process for creating this melding of business and people values within an organization is called the Shared Values Process, a major part of the Operating System.

To test the worth of the Operating System for business, we've funded third-party research since 1989 to gather before-and-after data. Improvements in communication, leadership, general wellness, and financial improvements have been quantified.

The best proof, however, comes not from research, but from the battlefield of business. In spring 1993, a crisis hit ALPAC Corporation, the Northwest Pepsi Cola operation, in the form of a syringe scare. A medical needle was found in a Diet Pepsi can. It quickly spread into an international event. By the next day, a second consumer reported finding a syringe. By Tuesday of the following week, 60 separate sightings of syringes in cans were reported in 20 states.

What could have ended in economic tragedy ended in triumph. Why did things go so well in handling this scare? Pepsi executives had prepared plans for just such a situation. *Advertising Age* said of this Pepsi needle hoax: "Perhaps more fundamental were long-running initiatives that empowered employees to act on well-defined values, emphasizing teamwork and high quality standards. Among the stated values of the Northwest bottler: 'Treat others with uncompromising truth' and 'Put the interests of others before your own.' In the end, what mattered most was an ingrained organizational commitment."

Where did this commitment come from? It came about because in 1990 ALPAC executives were trained in the Shared Values Operating System.

Adhering to shared values will help you focus on primary issues, reduce false starts, contribute more, retain staff, clarify your new culture, pull people together, clarify working relationships, and reduce politics and turf-building. It will help create an organization where experience and tradition can mix safely with new ideas and concepts. Even organizations under enormous stress experiencing downsizing, market reversals, or financial pressures—will benefit greatly because the Shared Values Operating System dramatically helps the healing process.

The Shared Values Process can help you build relationships of trust, communication, and openness. The Heroic Environment is a place you can call home.

Rob Lebow, author of Journey into the Heroic Environment, *and* Lasting Change, *is founder and chairman of The Lebow Company in Bellevue, Washington.*

Chapter 17

The Ethical Health of America

By David T. Kearns

I worry if America is going to lead the world in the 21st century. I ask: "Will our children have the skills they need to lead? Will they have the values? Will they have the ability to compete?" I am concerned because the next generation does not yet have the best schools in the world, they may not be learning the values they need to lead, and we as adults could be doing more to solve these problems. This is not about what kind of family we live in or which lifestyle is better. It's about what each of us needs to do as individuals to give all of our children every opportunity to succeed in a rapidly changing world.

America was built upon fundamental values. We declared our independence because of our conviction that "All men are created equal," and have "the right to life, liberty, and the pursuit of happiness." Men and women gave their lives so that future generations could enjoy these same individual rights and responsibilities.

Honesty, fairness, equality, courage, loyalty, kindness, hard work, and respect: these are the ethics that have been the foundation of our nation for over 200 years, and those are principles upon which we can all agree. They are timeless virtues that govern the way we act, the way we do business, and the way we treat others. They are the underpinnings of our freedom because our founding fathers knew such qualities are essential—that they were stars by which to set the new nation's course.

Thomas Jefferson understood that the key to these values was education. He wrote, "If a nation expects to be ignorant and free, it expects what never was and never will be." He wrote about the need to develop in students the ethics that he believed every citizen in a democracy needed to have. These values, he knew, were the keys to liberty and justice for all. In this nation, supreme power is vested in the people, and being well educated and sharing these values is integral to being a good citizen and maintaining the republic.

The key to these values remains education. We are not born with values. They are taught, learned, and practiced. Education is a lifelong process, and we develop over time the virtues that govern our actions. Children are always learning, by what they see and what they do. They learn all the time—at home, in school, on the playground, and in our neighborhoods. And they learn by example—by the way we act as adults, by the way we conduct our businesses, and the way we treat each other. Learning and citizenship go together.

Often, children grow up learning the wrong lessons when their environment is filled with crack addicts, drug dealers, and unscrupulous businessmen. They develop their ethics from what they see, and much of what they see on the streets, on TV, and in the news compounds the problem. In today's world, you have to be looking to see fundamental positive values in action.

Two Common Concerns

When we discuss our children and values, two common sentiments continuously come up: first, that schools shouldn't teach values; and second, if they do, they should teach them all and let the children decide what's best. Let me address both.

• *First, America somehow convinced itself that it wasn't fashionable or politically correct to teach values in our schools.* The bottom line is that all of our schools already teach values. They teach them every day in every class just like the rest of the world. To say that we shouldn't teach values in schools ignores the fact that our children learn life's lessons there anyway, and suggests that fundamental values we all share aren't worth teaching. So let's recognize that values are taught and learned, and focus on the ones that matter. I am not talking about teaching religious doctrine or personal preferences, but basic ethics that everyone needs.

The timeless values that built this country are those that matter the most. Former Secretary of Education, Bill Bennett, describes the process very simply:

"Do we want to teach our children about honesty? Then we might teach them about Abe Lincoln walking three miles to return six cents. Do we want children to know what courage means? Then we should teach them about Joan of Arc, Harriet Tubman, and the Underground Railroad. Do we want them to know about kindness and compassion, and their opposites? Then they should read A Christmas Carol *and* The Diary of Anne Frank. *We want them to know about hard work, so we should teach them about the Wright*

Brothers, and *Booker T. Washington learning to read. And if we want our children to learn to respect the rights of others, they should read* The Bill of Rights, *and Martin Luther King's* Letter from Birmingham Jail."

These lessons are neither complicated nor hard, nor should they be controversial.

• *Second, there is no such thing as a value-neutral education.* Everything is not relative—there are plenty of constants in our American values. Truth is better than dishonesty. Fairness is better than prejudice. We don't support the values of bigots, criminals, and sexists, and we don't support teaching their way of life. If you exclude values from schools, you will only teach that values aren't important. You send the message that the foundation of America isn't worth teaching, and provide no alternative to what our children see on TV. Yes, children will decide what values are important to them, but they need to know what values are important to us and why.

I was encouraged to see that the first thing Los Angeles area school superintendents did in response to the riots was begin to develop a values curriculum for all students.

Across America people are beginning another revolution—a revolution to rebuild our communities, reform our schools, and share our values. People are recognizing that to restore our values, we must restore our communities. Communities are formed by people who share common principles, respect, responsibility, and a sense of belonging. It is here that we must turn to ensure the education of our children. Our communities must agree to come together to take responsibility for the upbringing of our children.

Education is serving as the catalyst to bring us together to change our country. Education should not be treated as another social issue; it is the solution to a whole set of challenges we face, including our ethical health. People are beginning to recognize that our schools and our communities need to be rebuilt. People are beginning to recognize that ethics need to be taught in our schools—that values, schools, and communities go hand in hand.

The Leader's Charge

None of this will take place without leadership. As businessmen and women, we have a responsibility to embrace this role in restoring our communities and to lead this revolution.

First, we lead by example in our business practice. Just as there is no such thing as a values-neutral school, there is no such thing as a values-neutral company. You either promote good ethics, or you allow bad ethics to develop. A company's ethics are reflected in the rules that govern its business, like fairness and competition. As a young salesman at IBM, I was indoctrinated with the business ethics that governed that company and expected to apply them in everything I did. A company's ethics are reflected in the people it employs, the opportunities it provides them through training and services, and in the way it conducts internal business. Your employees learn from your corporate ethics, and they take their lead from your management and business processes.

As the leader of his or her company, the CEO has a responsibility to set the pace and the standard. For many, that means countless hours working to bring about systemic change in our education system at the state and community level. Similarly, as leaders in your community, you and your company have a responsibility to lead the revolution. While many read about revolutions, few participate. You have that opportunity and that responsibility.

We must take a stand and recognize that values need to be taught, and that they can and should be taught in school. We should recognize that we need to restore our communities because our schools can't do it all. We need to recognize that no one is going to do this for us, and so we are each going to have to take ownership ourselves. We should recognize that our businesses have a leadership responsibility and embrace it with action.

David Kearns prepared these remarks for the Ethics Resource Center's Pace Distinguished Lecture on Leadership in Ethics, endowed by General Dynamics and delivered at the Business Week *Symposium of CEOs. Based in Washington, D.C., the Center develops Character Education programs for schools.*

Chapter 18

Ethical Excellence

By Andrew Sikula, Sr.

*M*any executives involved in crimes often feel no remorse: *they feel their only mistake was getting caught.* Why are business ethics dangerously low or even disgustingly lacking?

Part of the problem is that winning is embedded in the American culture, attitude, and experience—and winning can't take place among equals. By nature, people want to be bigger, stronger, smarter, faster, prettier, and more successful than their peers. This often results in a win-at-any-cost mentality, even if cheating is involved. Sometimes this will to win is mistaken for a search for excellence. But a win-at-any-cost mentality results in moral decadence, not excellence.

Another reason for unethical behavior is the lack of linkage between ethical theory and practice. Much precept from philosophy and religion exists, but application to the real world leaves much to be desired. To fill the void, we need a "morality bridge"—an ethics standard and guide for individual behavior and corporate activity.

Four Master Principles

How can we replace decadence with development? We need a bridge to gain passage over the abyss, to get from a point of moral morass to the position of moral management. This involves the step-by-step implementation of four master principles.

• *Dignity.* All human beings have both intrinsic and extrinsic value and should be treated with courtesy and respect. People possess abilities and talents deserving of merit. Every individual has a quality or sum of qualities rendering him or her important, valuable, and useful. In addition, people have a character or quality of being honorable and noble—an inherent grace and stateliness. Even though such qualities may be dormant or underdeveloped, treat people with decorum, politeness, and respect.

• *Scrutiny.* Any decision made, any matter spoken or written, and all actions taken, must withstand close scrutiny, media attention, societal examination, and public appraisal. Executives should assume that their behaviors will be subject to media coverage and public debate. Having front-page newspaper coverage or prime-time television reports on your behavior is a good test of the wisdom of your decision or action. Power and position invite publicity and scrutiny. If your behavior can't withstand public scrutiny, you ought to change your behavior.

• *Humanity.* All human behavior should render meaningful benefit or contribution to humanity and the community. Such contribution causes the society in general to gain, advance, or develop. Significant societal service is a constructive but difficult requirement to fulfill on the way to moral maximization because it is threefold in nature: behaviors must be significant or meaningful; they must benefit society; and they must also make a contribution to humanity.

• *Accountability.* This principle suggests that ultimately some person or entity has final authority and power and will eventually judge the morality of one's thoughts (ideas), decisions, and actions. The "final authority" figure to whom one is responsible, answerable, and explainable may be God, conscience, the public, or one's constituency. People have both an obligation to perform and a requirement to report to this final authority figure who is the last element in a process, the highest judgment. Issues at this point are incapable of being further analyzed or divided. Ultimate accountability is a decisive principle—it is final, absolute, fundamental, and supreme.

While executives must adopt all four principles if they hope to attain moral management, the accountability standard or benchmark is the most difficult test. Ultimate accountability is the only principle which can substitute for the other three as the main gate and master determinant of moral management.

If implemented sequentially and collectively, these four principles result in "moral maximization"—behaviors, actions, and decisions resulting in the greatest advancement of individual and collective human rights, freedoms, equity, and development.

The Morality Bridge

Moral maximization is not a black-or-white issue—it is applied and implemented in degrees. Moral morass is the absence and moral management the presence of moral maximization. Sadly, moral management is often the "ideal" theory, but moral morass is the "real" practice.

The four master principles—which collectively make up the morality bridge—act as a rudder which steers human thoughts, decisions, and actions toward moral maximization and moral management. The more we navigate using the four principles, the closer we come to the ideal of moral management.

The morality bridge serves as a transition, passage, and movement from moral morass to moral management. Moral management advances human *rights, freedoms, equity* and *development.* Sometimes we find it tough to determine if a human thought, decision, or action will advance or retard these four conditions. To the degree that these conditions are satisfied determines the extent of the implementation of moral maximization.

We are presently in the condition of moral morass, moving toward moral decadence. Typically, moral decadence proceeds fast and easily. It involves travelling the lower level of the morality bridge—and this traffic flow is not blocked or restrained by moral principles. By contrast, moral development is slow. It involves taking the upper level of the morality bridge, passing through the four bridge parts and four master principles. Traffic from the lower level can be switched to the upper level and reversed in flow when a principle morally impacts a human thought, behavior, or action on the road toward moral management.

Andrew Sikula, Sr., is a Professor of Management at California State University, Chico, California.

Chapter 19

Vision, Mission, Values

By Jesse Stoner

*F*or many of us, vision seems elusive or unnecessary. However, vision does not have to be something magical or intangible—bestowed only by great leaders. Each of us is capable of creating a compelling vision and bringing it to reality. And when a group of people within a company share a common vision, amazing things happen.

Vision

Vision is a "picture of a highly desirable future state—a picture of the end result, not the process for getting there." It is more specific and tangible than just a vague sense of "positive thinking." At Ford Motor Company, "Job One" is the prototype that comes off the assembly line. It has to be perfect because it is the model that all others are built against. At Ford, "Quality is Job One" creates a clear vision of what quality looks like.

When people share a common vision, they share the same picture of success. For example, the shared vision at CNN is for the network to be viewed in every country in the world in English as well as the language of that region. It will be easy for all members of CNN to identify how close they are to achieving their desired future state.

Having a picture of the end-result creates tremendous energy. Consider the vision of the Apollo Moon project: "to place a man on the moon by the end of 1969." This clear picture generated and focused an incredible amount of energy. When they began the project, the technology to achieve it was not even in place. However, they overcame seemingly insurmountable obstacles, and their performance was outstanding and spectacular.

Mission

Vision alone is not enough to guide people in organizations toward the future. They must also understand the purpose or mission. Why did we want to place a man on the moon by the end of the decade in the 1960's? Was it to win the space race? To begin the Star Wars initiative? Or, in the spirit of "Star Trek," to boldly go where no one has gone before? Lacking a clear statement of purpose, (to answer "What next?") NASA has shown neither clear direction nor outstanding performance since 1970.

Mission is "a clear statement of purpose that explains your reason for existence." It answers the question "why." It is most powerful when it comes from your customer's perspective; not from the perspective of the services and products you offer.

Mary Parker Follett, a pioneering business consultant, was asked to help a troubled window shade company. The company's thinking was narrow and limited. When asked to define their business they said, "We produce window shades." When pressed to define what business they were really in, they discovered, "We are actually in the light control business." When considering their business from the viewpoint of their customers, they realized people who buy window shades really want to control the amount of light coming through their windows. This opened up new opportunities for producing and selling because there are many ways to control light.

Stanley Magic Door could have decided they were in the business of making automatic doors. Instead, they defined themselves as in the business of "facilitating and controlling the access of people and things through buildings." What a difference in implications for future directions! And, their people have a greater understanding and excitement for the products they produce and sell.

According to Disney, their purpose is to "use our imagination to bring happiness to millions." Merck researches and produces drugs; however, their purpose is to "preserve and improve human life."

Values

Clear purpose alone will not create the future you desire. Clear purpose tells what you do, but it does not give any guidelines for how this purpose is to be accomplished. Clearly stating and living your values fuels the passion that keeps you focused in the face of obstacles, adversity, and change. Values tap into people's feelings. They evolve standards people care deeply about.

A value is a deeply held and enduring view of what we believe is worthwhile. Values specify in broad, general ways how we will achieve our vision. They describe how we intend to operate, on a day-to-day basis, as we pursue our vision.

Consider the vision of Chemlawn; "Making America green one lawn at a time." How much stronger would it be if it included operating values like "in an environmentally safe manner."

You Need It All—One Statement

Neither mission, values, or vision alone can guide people. You need a statement that includes all three. When you can make one statement that encompasses all, a tremendous amount of energy is suddenly unleashed. There is a higher level of commitment because employees are able to see the relationship between the direction of their company and what they personally believe in and care deeply about. It ensures that all employees are quite clear about what they are doing, why they are doing it, and how their work relates.

Henry Ford envisioned the common people driving around in automobiles. He saw access of everyone, not just the elite. The mission for his company was to build and make available affordable transportation (automobiles). The underlying values were to create access for everyone, not just the rich. The vision of the end result was of a multitude of cars on the road, driven by all kinds of people. As his vision became clear, the means to achieve it also became clear; and eventually he developed a way to achieve it—mass production.

Compelling visions are about more than just survival. They are about being great, going for the gold, and stretching beyond what is easily achievable.

Is your company's vision statement clear, understandable, believable, challenging, enduring? Is it about being great—not solely about beating the competition? Is it inspiring—not expressed solely in numbers? Does it provide guidelines that help you make daily business decisions? Can each person in the company find himself or herself in it and see where he or she fits?

The most powerful strategy is *commitment*. Sometimes people mistakenly think they want something, only to find that they cannot commit or get excited about it. Once you develop your vision, choose it. Choosing means commitment. Commitment means power. The power of commitment begins when you take action.

Jesse Stoner is the author of Creating Your Organization's Future, *a program designed to help members of teams and organizations create a shared vision, mission, and values, and the strategies to achieve them.*

Chapter 20

Due Process

By Charles E. Watson

If an organization does not have a comprehensive code of ethics or if those in power lack moral fiber and allow the arbitrary imposition of unwritten regulations, grave injustices can easily occur—particularly when leaders are naive when it comes to matters of the law.

Even a small sample of life experience will tell us that all people do not get along. Indeed, we all have a tendency to rub someone else the wrong way. In every organization, there is at least one person whom someone else would like to "put in his place" or dispose of altogether. One way is to charge the offensive party with the high crime of ethical misconduct.

Guilty by Implication

Suppose a man named Jones is seen as a nuisance by his manager. How do the anti-Jones forces deal with him? The first step is natural and easy. They speak ill of Jones and get others to join their "get Jones" campaign. Gossip starts to flow: "Well," someone says, "I heard this of Jones. Did you know he actually did that, or he said this?" Soon, scores of people, some who once liked Jones, see him as not just weird but evil. He must be disposed of and the sooner the better.

The anti-Jones band now looks high and low for something, anything, Jones said or did that, in their opinion, is wrong. This is not an organized effort; nonetheless, it evolves. Many now take a hand at snooping into all phases of Jones's life, searching to find offenses. And, they find some. Jones is like everyone else—he's no saint. The witch hunt is on.

Word of further offenses intensifies their efforts. His boss tricks the unsuspecting Jones into tattling on himself, revealing small indiscretions he—like practically everyone else—has committed. The list of

Jones's misdeeds grow. Before long charges are drawn up against him. Even though these are not specific violations of the ethics code, the charges appear to have merit. On the surface they make Jones out to be a bad apple who must be plucked from the barrel and tossed away.

The "get Jones" movement peaks when formal charges of wrongdoing are brought before the authorities. Top leadership has no particular axe to grind with Jones. But as they see it, the power structure must be preserved, and this means supporting those lower down in the chain of command. If his supervisor says Jones is guilty, then they'll go along with it. Besides, Jones is a nobody—so to hell with what's true or fair. Dismissal proceedings are initiated against Jones. If he can't convince an appeals panel of his innocence, he's gone—terminated.

Jones must face a formal hearing to clear himself of a long list of allegations. His job is on the line, and he's terrified. He doesn't understand how the system works or exactly why he is a victim of it. He looks for help. A friend suggests he get a lawyer, and Jones hires one to represent him. The organization has a full-time attorney on its payroll to represent it, but Jones has to pay his lawyer himself. The playing field isn't level, but that's Jones's problem. Even if Jones "wins" his case, he still loses! His legal fees run into the tens of thousands of dollars—far more than the fines levied against convicted felons.

Appeals are heard by a panel of one's peers—others in the organization elected to decide and recommend to the top brass what should be done. Now what takes place in the minds and actions of the panelists is remarkable—and frightening. Elected to safeguard the rights of other employees and ensure justice, these ordinary folks somehow forget that they are human; they begin to see themselves as judges. In their minds, they are a good bit purer than Jones or anyone else who might come before them. So, they look at every scrap of evidence against Jones with moral outrage. As they see things, it is Jones who is unclean. Moreover, the appeals panel is of a mind to follow its own methods for handling the case. One of them says, "Let's not get too legalistic." Disregard for the legal system and its ideals and safeguards creeps in.

What Jones is accused of is little different than what others have done; but others aren't unpopular with management as Jones is. And everyone whispers to himself, "What's happening to Jones would never happen to me because I'm liked around here." None of the panel members are the slightest bit concerned about the pain Jones is experiencing because they do not regard Jones as a human being with fears and feelings—just a scoundrel who has brought on his own troubles.

Jones is accused of many violations. Some allegations have a small measure of truth to them. After all, Jones is no saint. The appeals panel begins to find fault with Jones, not because he has broken established rules but because he isn't flawless. Worse yet, the charges brought against Jones are for offenses not mentioned in the organization's code of conduct, but offenses broadly labeled as ethical misconduct—what the "get Jones" gang says are a breech of professional ethics. As the hearing progresses further and other witnesses speak, additional allegations of evil doing by Jones come to light, and he must answer to these.

To top it all off, dirty tricks used by the "get Jones" gang are brought to light during the hearing. They are deplorable if not illegal. But the reaction by top management and the appeals panel is, "So what? Jones is the one on trial, not his accusers." Sadly, top management lacks the moral fiber to intervene. Jones is a victim of lawlessness disguised as discipline for ethical infractions, and there is no defense against this sort of thing.

Basic Rights Under Law

Every citizen has the right to life, liberty, and the pursuit of happiness. This means the right to earn a living—something that would be unjustly denied a person found guilty of trumped-up ethical violations. We are all better off when basic rights are respected and our disputes are settled by laws and not by power or the prevailing mood. This means that people should be punished only for infractions of codified laws, not for actions that annoy or offend others because they are not politically correct at the moment, or for "crimes," so defined, after the fact. Ideally, penalties should be clearly established for each offense, beforehand, and not concocted on the spot. Fishing expeditions to identify wrongdoing of any sort violate our right to privacy; they are harassing because they always succeed in finding minuscule wrongs—no one is perfect. Everyone is entitled to due process. This means legal representation and a fair and impartial hearing where specific charges must be proven beyond a reasonable doubt before a guilty verdict is pronounced.

The best way to make the work-place discipline process ethical is to keep it legal—to follow standard legal procedures and traditions. The only thing that protects each of us from the injustices that befell Jones is the law. We all will annoy someone at one time or another, and without the law we can easily slip to an inhumane level. Indeed, the law not only protects our rights but more importantly it protects us from each other.

Charles E. Watson is a professor of management at the Richard T. Farmer School of Business Administration, Miami University Ohio.

Section III

How Are Ethics Applied?

Chapter 21

The Ethics Umbrella

By Shannon Bellamy

*M*ost business people are hardworking individuals who believe in their company's product, are trying to make an honest living, and want to produce a fair profit for their company. They generally want to be good people and do good things. Yet, even these people make unethical choices. How are we to account for these mistakes?

Unless we discover the origin of these errors, we won't know how to solve the problems. Is the main source of these mistakes similar to some math problem errors in that people are just "sloppy" in their ethical calculations? Perhaps they have just forgotten how to do some "ethical calculation"? Is it more the case that they fail to recognize the situation at hand as being one belonging to the discipline of business ethics? Which is it: a failure of perception or one of judgment.

My conclusion is that people generally are unethical not because they fail to make the correct ethical "calculation" but rather they do not even perceive that the situation confronting them even comes under the rubric of ethics.

For example, they may full well see the marketing dimensions of the situation, or the financial considerations, or accounting ramifications, but they either fail to perceive sufficient ethical detail of the problem before them or they fail to perceive that there are any ethical considerations at all.

Much like the person who blindly runs a red light, they do not even see the oncoming "ethical" traffic until it is too late, until they are hit—hit, for example, with their first and career-ending sexual harassment suit. The person who at least perceived the light being "ethically" red in the first place has many more alternatives available. They can brace for the impact, try to avoid the collision, warn their fellow passengers, or come to a safe stop and avoid any problems at all.

The first step in any ethics intervention program is to *increase one's awareness of the ethical dimensions of decision making.* Most business ethics training does not effectively do this. Instead ethics training often requires people to render judgments on pre-packaged cases, such as "whistleblowing" in which the ethical dilemma has already been outlined, discovered, perceived, and resolved. Real-life ethical problems do not come so neatly packaged and labeled. To be as the American author Henry James said, "richly aware and finely responsible" requires a fair amount of ethical sensitivity and creativity—and work.

Uses of the Umbrella

The metaphor of the Ethics Umbrella has great appeal and application. I see 10 areas where this metaphor can re-shape, expand, and positively enhance our ethical thinking.

• *Personal.* Holding an umbrella is personal. It requires personal responsibility. If we do not want to get wet, then we must hold the umbrella. No one can do it for us. This serves as a reminder that ethics is not just some abstract theory but is always in some person's hands.

• *Strength.* You have probably seen umbrellas which collapse under certain weather conditions. Like the weather, business conditions do get rough at times, and one's ethical umbrella needs to be up to the task at hand; otherwise, you will get swept away with the storm. The strength of the umbrella is a metaphor for the strength of one's character. Lightweight ethics get blown away in rough times.

• *Integrity.* An umbrella needs to be strong, but it needs to be strong in a certain way. The spines all need to be strong as one another, and the handle needs to be well integrated with the spines. A single weak spine can ruin an otherwise good umbrella. The umbrella needs to function smoothly, opening and closing with ease and be in balance, just like one's ethical character. Courage, honesty, discretion, and loyalty are all personal virtues, but like the spines of the umbrellas they only function well if they are in balance with the rest of the umbrella. The Ethics Umbrella encourages us to lead an integrated ethical life.

• *Inclusiveness.* Often we fail to consider how our actions will affect others. We leave them out in the rain, so to speak. Including ourselves and others under the Ethics Umbrella gives everyone a better opportunity.

• *Clarity.* Situations that lie outside the umbrella are obscured by the rain. When we bring them under the umbrella, we can see what they are and what decisions are appropriate.

• *Protection.* To paraphrase Thomas Hobbes, the 17th century writer, without ethics life would be "short, brutish, and ugly." The Ethics Umbrella provides protection for all those underneath it.

• *Timeliness.* If it rained all the time, we would use umbrellas all the time. Luckily, it does not. Likewise, it does not "ethically" rain all the time either, and so we do not always use our Ethics Umbrellas. Fortunately, most decisions are made with clear vision on sunny days. But should we need it, we know the umbrella is available. When the weather is marginal, it always best to pack your umbrella!

• *Enabling.* Ethics is often thought of as a list of prohibitions: *don't do this and don't do that.* Many people believe they could make more money if they did not have to be ethical. The umbrella metaphor avoids some of these negative connotations. The Ethics Umbrella is an enabling device that helps us all get what we want in a cooperative manner.

• *Styles.* Umbrellas come in many different styles according to individual needs and preferences, but they all have the same general shape and function. People too, have different ethical styles. While we may not always like the size, shape, or color of their umbrellas, we should tolerate those individual differences—if the style is still ethical. For example, egoism is an ethical style. It has room under it for only one person, the owner, and therefore fails to include others.

• *Action.* Some people own very functional umbrellas, but they fail to use them. Ethics Umbrellas, like real ones, only work if we put them up. They do no good if we refuse to use them. The Ethics Umbrella should be ready for action, whether one is at work, at home, or at play. Ethics takes action!

• *Singularity.* Most of us have only one umbrella. We take it with us wherever we go. We pack it in our car or in our briefcase. We use it at work, at home, at play. It would be confusing and difficult to have different umbrellas for different occasions. Ethics is similar. It is much simpler to have one good, sturdy Ethics Umbrella—one that works wherever we go. Having different Ethics Umbrellas for work and private life would require changing umbrellas so often that one would develop a sort of ethical schizophrenia.

The Ethics Umbrella, when properly deployed, can enable both organizations and individuals to see the ethical terrain more clearly.

Shannon Bellamy is a business ethicist in Midvale, Utah.

Chapter 22

Ethical Approach to Business

By Larry Colero

Studies show strong correlations between a company's standards of integrity and successful business transactions. The establishment of trust, based on an ethical reputation, allows a business to form and maintain long-term productive relationships with its clients, suppliers, and staff. When there are no clear-cut answers, dialogue on ethical dilemmas is the key to moral conduct. Through open dialogue, a common understanding of ethical choices can be reached.

In the pursuit of profit, business leaders need to safeguard the welfare of staff, community, and other stakeholders. They can not afford to exploit human resources, or extract natural resources at any cost. Fortunately, ethical business is often more profitable. For example, the customer's perception that a company is concerned about the environment is an important part of the success of any product. No longer do negotiators promote a win-at-all-costs approach.

Business people are often perceived (and portrayed) as shortsighted, greedy, and uncaring. Whether or not this is true, business leaders need to move toward a stance of honesty, respect for individual rights, and stewardship of nature—for their own good, as well as the good of others. Even though many professional associations have codes of ethics, these normally dictate individual behavior within the context of professional practice (law, medicine, engineering). There is a pressing need to ensure that organizations exemplify responsible behavior. This is why companies develop codes of ethics.

Shades of Gray

Ethical decisions in business are often difficult to make. The challenge of applying ethical considerations is two-fold: first, the "right" thing to do is usually a matter of opinion, particularly in the cultural diversity of today's world economy; and second, even if there is agreement on the right thing, it may not be possible under the circumstances, due to its adverse effect on something else. This is what you might call an ethical trade-off. There is nothing underhanded or even unconscionable in the intent. It is simply a case of choosing between the lesser of two evils.

I find it useful to think of ethical behavior in four categories:

• *Goodwill—benevolence or stewardship.* The goal is always to strive for goodwill to all concerned. Albert Einstein said, "Concern for man himself and his fate must always form the chief interest of all technical endeavors." Similarly, in business there can be a higher purpose than a simple profit motive.

• *Ethical trade-off—an informed choice between alternatives.* If immediate goodwill is not possible, then a conscious decision can be made to do the best possible thing under the circumstances (ethical trade-off). A critical factor in an ethical trade-off is the completeness of the information considered. There is little room for posturing or defensiveness.

• *Honest intent—unintentional damage to the welfare of others.* This may result from a lack of information or a lack of awareness of the full impact of actions taken. Unfortunately, it is often caused by a propensity to rationalize unethical behavior. Honest intent often occurs in large organizations where functions are specialized, or in situations where someone or something else does the work and the decision-maker is not personally on site to witness the full effect of a decision. On the surface, honest intent appears as indifference—ethical issues are not even considered or discussed. For example, employees tend to unwittingly relinquish the responsibility for ethical choices. Instead of individual consciences being combined, they are somehow lost altogether, as no one individual takes personal responsibility for the hardship caused to others. Honest intent can take many insidious forms, and the end result is usually a numbed conscience.

• *Malice—willful harm inflicted upon others.* Purely unethical behavior is knowing that someone is being harmed, but failing to prevent it for selfish reasons. Malice is the conscious intent to breach ethical responsibilities. Unfortunately, murderous profiteering still exists in the international business community. For example, child slavery is common in the Third World.

Business decisions can be weighed within the context of these four categories to decide what is needed (more information, greater awareness, or enforcement) and what action to take.

Ethical behavior is based upon a concern for the welfare of others. This concern stems from an active personal conscience. Ethical considerations must be given priority in the course of managing a business.

Larry Colero is president of Crossroads Consulting, Delta, B.C., Canada.

Chapter 23

Being Ethical

By Gregory A. Gull

*S*ince we all seek to make right decisions, we each live our lives based upon principles we believe to be true: we make decisions consistent with our beliefs. Many executives believe the business of business is profit, not the morality of society. According to this point of view, it is government's role to be the gatekeeper of morality, to discover the need for laws, create laws, and enforce laws that will ensure a moral society. They think that ethical conduct of business is conduct that is within the law and that ethics is an individual thing—after all, it is people's behavior that is unethical.

Today, many organizations are realizing the cost of just staying within the law, and not being ethical, is too great. Many realize that, unethical behavior is detrimental to lasting success. Many managers view ethics as another discipline or functional area that is to be controlled; not unlike marketing, sales, manufacturing, and finance. Not surprisingly, many in management deal with ethical problems in the same manner as they do quality problems; they seek conformity to externally imposed standards. In effect, they institute more stringent rules, develop training programs, design an inspection (control) process, and enforce their standards by chasing down each occurrence of unethical behavior as if each is special—as if each is an independent result of someone else's "human error."

Managing ethics in this way will always be problematic, for it erroneously assumes that people behave in a vacuum; that the observed behavior is independent of the environment within which it occurs or from which it emanates. Holding onto this perspective keeps many people in management from taking responsibility for their involvement and participation in the unethical practices of their organization. People with this perspective tend to view ethics as another bothersome aspect of doing business. They see it, like quality, as yet another thing they must comply with that only adds to the cost of doing business.

To be ethical is to understand the difference between right and wrong and to act accordingly. However, one cannot assess right from wrong without having an intent in mind; right versus wrong can only be assessed in relation to a system of values. This does not mean that ethics is a relativistic concept. If it is, we could not say an act is wrong, for our belief in ethical relativism would necessitate us being accepting of all value systems. But, obviously, this is not the case. There is something in all of us that informs us of what is right for all of us. Since we abhor the exploitation and manipulation of life, we recognize the existence of a universal set of values that are applicable to all. Ethics has to do with what is common to all of us; it concerns what is inherent in our nature.

Clearly, ethics has no meaning in a world of things, for ethics addresses the fundamental issues of life: meaning and self-preservation. Thus, to speak of ethical behavior is to speak of behavior that is consistent with life-affirming values—values that are in harmony with the nature of all that is alive. To be ethical is to make choices consistent with life-centered values and not to be guided by values that are external to life.

We mistakenly advance the belief that there are different values for the different roles we assume in life. Consequently, the decisions we make in our role as a business person reference a different set of values than the values we reference in our role as a parent or friend. While we would disapprove of those who would unload their children or friends in an attempt to maximize their position or disposable income, we applaud the same decision in business. Sadly, we are oblivious to the contradiction.

We believe life is divisible, and then we wonder why realizing ethical behavior is problematic. The more our values in professional or business life differ from the life-centered values inherent in our nature, the more unethical our organizations and society will become. The more discordant the set of values, the greater the likelihood that ethical problems will occur. Since people cannot live a divided life and remain sane, many become numb to their (inherent) personal values to avoid feeling troubled over the contradiction. Thus, the mentality of the herd prevails over reason as a guide.

The principles upon which our businesses are run are inseparable from the principles upon which we live our lives. Unfortunately, traditional neo-classical business practices don't enhance or promote our moral development—they curtail it. As we turn our attention toward the amassing of things, we lose touch with that which is alive; we become alienated from ourselves and each other. As alienation increases, we lose all perspective on living and, with it, our ability for ethical decision making decreases as we become more and more irresponsible. We become irresponsible when we disregard the long term—ignoring the far-reaching effects of a decision—for the sake of expediency and our selfish benefit in the short term. In effect, we misconstrue the means for living with the meaning of life; we confuse means and ends as we elevate our material desires to the status of a right.

If an organization is to remain viable, its behavior must become unquestionably ethical. Executives must be integrative in the decision-making process by taking a dynamic view when choosing a course of action. To this end, an organization's system must incorporate life-affirming values and the material needs of economic sustainability. In short, business must be practiced on the field of ethics, and not conversely, if the intent is to remain viable.

Gregory Gull, founder of Practicum Unlimited, provides eduction and consulting in Systemic Management and Leadership. Greg also facilitates learning in Ethics and Management in the accelerated degree program in Management at Rosemont College, Rosemont, Pennsylvania.

Chapter 24

Three Steps to Self-Integrity

By Genie Z. Laborde

We like simple mandates, and we think ethics should be simple. On the surface, "Love thy neighbor as thyself" sounds simple, but in reality, it's not. Many of us don't love ourselves much, and we love our neighbors even less—or not at all.

This mandate of *loving thy neighbor* is an example of the complexity of ethics, integrity, and being true to yourself.

These concepts are interrelated. Integrity is honesty with yourself and unity with yourself and others. We all have many sub-personalities (sets of learned behaviors), and these are often at war with one another: *I want to go, and I want to stay; I want to love, and I don't want to love; I want to succeed, and I want to take a year off.* These warring sub-personalities can lead to neurotic behaviors. When these sub-personalities are in agreement, we have unity or integrity with the "intrinsic knowing" of who we are and how we can best express this in action.

Martin Buber called this intrinsic knowing the "still small voice." Others have called it conscience, the higher self, the inner self, the core self. The important thing is to communicate with this "voice" or "self" because with its guidance you can discover levels of energy and experiences unavailable to others. The more time you spend in these enlightened states, the more you know yourself and express yourself with integrity. And the more personal power and earned self-esteem you will have.

So, how do you stay in this state of integrity? First, let us consider our basic needs. We all have needs which clamor to be filled. We have *physical needs* for food, shelter, and sex. We also have psychological needs for *identity* (the need to know yourself by what you like, what you dislike, what activities you are proud of, what doings you are ashamed of), for *connectedness* (the need to belong to a group, to hold close an idea, to love and be associated with others); and for *potency* (the need to have some impact on the things and people in our world).

Most behaviors are focused on filling one, two, or three of these needs. So, our process is to become aware of a need, satisfy the need, and remain content until a new need arises. When our behavior patterns allow us to fill these needs in a natural way, we are content. We feel united, and we have integrity.

When this process of need-awareness-satisfaction is interrupted, we are unhappy and frustrated. We sometimes try bizarre behaviors in an attempt to satisfy our needs. We lose our feeling of unity with ourselves and with the world. We do not feel in control of our lives. Sometimes we try to ignore our needs and engage in destructive behaviors because they distract us from this basic process.

Time to Ponder

Twelve years ago, I began studying a new discipline that attracted the sleaziest bunch of instructors and students I'd ever seen assembled in one classroom. This discipline was taught one weekend a month for seven months. After the first week, I dropped out because I didn't want to spend time with people like that. In class, I felt that I had to keep my hand on my purse. Most of the students were shifty-eyed, closed-mouthed, and interested in how to part people from their money. The smell of power emanating from the skills of this discipline attracted this kind of audience. It still does.

The following week I stopped a friend from committing suicide, using the one skill I learned the week before at the seminar. The faculty hadn't taught me "why" the skill worked; they'd only conveyed this simple technique to change one emotion to another emotion quickly. In this case, deep suicidal depression changed to creative excitement in response to touches and a few key words. This simple technique saved and changed my friend's life. I wanted to know "why" it worked, and I wanted to know more techniques. So, three weeks later, I was back in class, among the unwashed, unrepentant, and unethical.

During those weeks, I thought a lot about integrity, right and wrong, manipulation, and taking advantage of other people, including taking money by offering more than you can deliver. This idea of promising "blue sky" was the dominant conversation at seminar breaks. I was no longer worried about my purse, but about the future with 100 manipulators joyfully fleecing people, skillfully.

During the next two years, I continued to ponder integrity and ethics as I continued studying the discipline. I took a certain amount of ribbing from students and faculty about my determined "fairness." All my dealings had to be "fair," or I was uncomfortable. One founder of this discipline became my business partner, and he would tease me about this "fairness mania." He liked me, and tried to show me that my need for "fairness" made me vulnerable. I was unconvinced and watched him pay for his need to always win—to always get a trifle more for himself than was fair. He won short-term and lost long-term.

Three Steps to Take

By the time I wrote *Influencing with Integrity,* I'd discussed the difference between influencing and manipulating with thousands of people. I settled on a simple, three-part formula for influencing others with integrity.

1. Know your heart's desire. The first step toward operating from your core self is to find out, on a conscious here-and-now level, what it is you want. We all have needs, physical and psychological. These needs express themselves as a desire, a goal. Ask yourself, "What do I want now?" If you are at work and find yourself in a business interaction, take a break and ask yourself this question. Once you've answered your own question, then resume the interaction and find out what the other person wants from the meeting. If you have set up rapport with the other person, he or she will tell you the outcome, and together you can work on creative ways for both of you to get what you want. This is a win-win plus. In business, rapport can occur once trust in competence for the task at hand has been established. Eliciting someone's outcome or goal is an excellent way to establish rapport.

When you are seeking ways to obtain your goal and the goal of the other person, then you are acting with integrity. You are creating a unity with the other person in pursuit of a goal big enough to satisfy both of you.

2. Eliminate "shoulds." How do you know the "still small voice" is requesting a real intrinsic need and when is the need a bogus one—one learned from our culture and not really essential to you? If the need sounds like a "should" or a "should not," then this is not your core self speaking. This is a learned need and not really useful in satisfying core needs. If the need is a "desire," then this is the still small voice. One caveat: if the desire will hurt someone else—physically—this is not a core desire. If the desire will cause some psychological hurt to someone else, it may or may not be a core need. You need another litmus test. For example, some symbiotic relationships, like mother-daughter, need to be separated, and one may suffer the loss temporarily. The one who is ready to move out may need to do whatever is necessary to ease the separation, but some emotional pain may be inevitable for both to grow into maturity.

3. Engage in win-win plus creative thinking. To establish a winwin plus, we must find out others' hearts' desires and help them attain them. Most of us feel good when we are helping other people to attain their outcomes, especially if we are moving toward our own outcomes as well. When you are aware of your own heart's desire, your intuitive, intrinsic knowing about what's missing from your life, and you are helping another gain his or her own greatest need, then you are operating with integrity, and your own feeling of self-confidence will reflect this. You are expressing your own integrity. Enthusiasm, energy, motivation and personal power are the inevitable results.

Now that you have a definition of integrity and three simple steps to aid you in behaving with integrity, let the complexities come. The ancient Chinese philosophers had a term called "Te," pronounced "Der." "Te" means to be in the right place at the right time in the right frame of mind. This is integrity. If you follow the three steps of knowing your heart's desire, eliciting and helping others gain their need, and working toward a creative way to satisfy these collective needs, then you will experience the flow of integrity. You will be in the right place at the right time in the right frame of mind.

Genie Z. Laborde, author of Influencing with Integrity *and* Fine Tune Your Brain, *is president of International Dialogue Education Associates, a leader in the field of communications theory and its practical applications, Redwood City, California.*

Chapter 25

Managing Ethics

By Peter Madsen

*H*ow does one manage ethics? What steps can one take to institutionalize ethics within an organization? Many executives are taking the following ten steps. These steps suggest that there are practical measures for reducing scandal and corruption.

1. Leadership at the top. If ethics is to become a vital part of an organization, then the top managers must demonstrate their commitment in both word and deed. Nothing sends a signal to members louder than the CEO stating that he or she has a priority which should be addressed by everyone in the organization. CEOs and the other officers of an organization must articulate a vision that emphasizes the priority of ethics and ethical conduct. Silence on ethical issues can be deadly.

A statement of values and beliefs. One way for top management to articulate its leadership role is by means of an organizational statement of values and beliefs. These documents serve as directions to organizational members, as an orientation to new members, and as a centralized articulation of the shared values operative in the organization. Statements drafted by means of a survey have the advantage of being more readily acceptable, rather than those which are imposed in a "top-down" manner. They should express the basic purpose of the organization and the relative value that it places upon its relationships with groups both internal and external to the organization.

2. A code of conduct. Most organizations today have codes of conduct. They are specific, policy documents that cover the most fundamental areas of concern and should be well circulated throughout the organization. Codes can serve the purpose of guiding behavior and of clarifying responsibilities. Clear statements of disciplinary actions in case of violations should also be made in the code.

Topics covered in most organizational codes include: conflicts of interest, illegal conduct such as bribery or kickbacks, safeguarding company assets, honesty in organizational communications, whistle-blowing, gifts, entertainment and travel, proprietary information, governmental contracting responsibilities, drug and alcohol abuse, and sexual harassment.

3. *An ethics committee.* Many organizations have established ethics committees to oversee the effort to institutionalize ethics. Committees can be formed from the rank-and-file, or they can be established at the Board level. Many committees are chaired by the chief executive to further underscore the importance of ethics. The committee can serve in an advisory capacity or in a decision-making one. They can investigate cases as they arise within the organization and adjudicate them. They can devise policy and update the existing code of conduct from time to time. Their existence also sends a signal to employees that ethics is a serious issue within the organization.

4. *Ethics audits.* Ethics audits are being used more and more by executives to preempt ethical problems before they become troublesome. Auditing the internal environment can be useful to pinpoint trouble spots that might cause unethical conduct. Are codes and ethics policies specific and clear? Are they being followed, or is lip service to them the rule? Are ethically sensitive functional areas such as purchasing or sales being monitored adequately? Such an audit program can serve as an exercise in organizational development and augment the work of an ethics committee.

5. *Auditing the external environment is also useful to identify the social responsibilities of the organization.* Is there a negative impact on the environment? Has the organization been active in promoting the social good of its community? What is the track record on the hiring and promotion of minorities and women? When ethics audits are conducted, involve as many managers and employees as possible to underscore the importance that the organization places upon ethics.

6. *Appraising ethics on the job.* Annual appraisals can include a category for recognizing the quality of the individual employee's performance in the ethics area. Have they included ethical considerations in the decisions they make on the job? Have they brought up ethics as a concern in the planning of projects and tasks? What kind of role model for ethics has a manager been? Have they contributed to the general awareness of the importance of ethics on the part of their subordinates? Evaluating the character of individuals can serve as a reminder to them that conduct on the job is an important part of their career success.

7. *Communicating ethics.* If ethics is to flourish within an organization, then a program that communicates this goal must be established. Some use an annual "letter of representation" that requires certain managers to state that they do not have any conflict of interest, that they are familiar with the organization's code of conduct, and that they have abided by its provisions over the past year. Pamphlets, brochures, posters, articles, publications, videos, and memoranda that serve as reminders about ethical conduct are all possible vehicles in such a communications program. New policies in ethics or changes to existing ones need to be disseminated widely as well.

Broadcasting an organization's concern about ethics in a well-orchestrated communications program will have great effect on the way employees consider ethics in their daily decision making.

8. Reporting violations. Employees need to be encouraged to make voluntary reports of illegal, unethical, or questionable conduct that they witness on the job. This can be accomplished by including a provision in the code of conduct about making such reports and/or devising a corporate policy on whistleblowing.

Such a policy should include provisions about proper procedures, confidentiality and options for making anonymous reports, protections for people making reports, prohibitions of retaliation against those making reports, the need for documented evidence in the report, and the unacceptability of making frivolous reports. Many organizations have established a hotline telephone number which employees can call to make a voluntary report of wrongdoing. Once a report has been made, the organization should investigate and where necessary take appropriate actions, keeping the reporter of the event informed along the way.

9. Enforcing violations. If an organization takes the time and effort to devise an ethics program, it should take the time and effort to enforce any infractions of the policies or code that it devises. Nothing sends the wrong signal to employees like unenforced policies or codes. Violations are sure to increase if management "look the other way" when wrongdoing takes place. This is not to suggest, however, that executives enforce its ethics program without due process. Enforcement must be firm, but fair.

10. Training. A program of education and training is perhaps an important part of creating an environment for ethics and ethical conduct. The purpose of the ethics training program is not to moralize or preach but to empower people by helping them to identify their responsibilities and to assist them in making the hard ethical choices that they will face in their careers.

Such training is best done through an interactive training experience using case study analysis and discussions of situations relevant to the participants and their functional areas. New employee orientation, management and supervisory development programs and general ethics educational programs can be designed to help build the critical thinking skills necessary in the resolution of hard ethical dilemmas faced by employees on the job. Training can be useful, then, in addressing both "managerial mischief" and "moral mazes" in management.

These ten steps can be taken as organizational development strategies. Many might argue, however, that just as morality cannot be legislated by governments, executives can't order people to be ethical. Although there are never any guarantees that unethical or questionable practices can be eliminated from the workplace, these strategies will do much to build a workplace culture where ethical conduct is highly valued. The building of such a culture is one of the ethical responsibilities of the enlightened executive in search of organizational excellence.

Peter Madsen, Executive Director of the Center for the Advancement of Applied Ethics, Carnegie Mellon University, is co-editor of Essentials of Business Ethics. *He consults with and conducts ethics training programs for private, public and nonprofit organizations.*

Chapter 26

Giving Values a Voice

By Terry Mandel

We're on the brink of a global paradigm shift, and the systems orientation, basic to this new worldview, will enable us to reintegrate all that's been fragmented since the 17th century, when power eclipsed spirit as the currency of human exchange.

Far from discarding power, however, the new paradigm balances power with spirit, human invention with natural systems, image with substance. The iron grip of "either/or" is being softened by the healing salve of "both/and."

Making transitions from international to global markets, from multi-national to multicultural companies, from hierarchical to horizontal organizations, and from transactional to relational interactions is the first step toward applying the new principles in our work and lives.

Baby Boomers, now culture shapers as well as culture shakers, are bringing the values of the '60s into the new century. The widespread acceptance of participative management, ESOPs, intuition in the workplace, flextime, and socially responsible business practices parallel the Boomers' rise. In spite of this generation's growing influence, however, one arena remains virtually unchanged: marketing.

The Heart of Marketing

Even people committed to values-based management often use traditional marketing strategies that play on people's fantasies and fears. The antidote to this cynicism and stagnation is a new model of marketing that mirrors the new paradigm. Instead of discounting marketing as merely a vehicle of information, we can learn to use it as a tool for transformation. Admittedly, this requires something of a leap. Most advertising is insulting, much of the junk we get in the mail is junk, and many salespeople are intrusive. But what has been sullied in the name of greed can be reborn in the service of truth.

Freed from the stigma of how others use or abuse it, marketing offers us the power to give voice to that which most inspires and moves us in our work. When we share our visions, we build bridges.

Most people think *marketing with integrity* is an oxymoron, like *jumbo shrimp*, or *honest politician*. But this new paradigm of marketing speaks to the possibility that we can successfully promote ourselves and our ideas and profitably sell our products and services in ways that are consistent with our individual and corporate styles, values, and intentions.

What is marketing, if not a process we use, consciously or unconsciously, to communicate our values? We market with integrity when we balance our attitudes and actions with our values and vision. Surprisingly, the result is a competitive advantage that can raise the standard of operation within an industry while rewarding everyone involved with a greater sense of purpose.

This redefinition shifts the focus of marketing from the organization outward to include the inner organization, as well. By building a bridge between inner and outer worlds—within ourselves as much as in our companies—we make possible the integration of our values and actions, our inspiration and expression, our work and spirit.

Marketing with integrity creates a context in which an authentic and abiding relationship is not only possible, but very nearly irresistible. The dark side of that ideal is the false chumminess and relentless pushiness that characterize traditional marketing and advertising. The safeguard for that is integrity, which is not about moral superiority or perfection, but about balance and wholeness. Marketing has untapped potential for making a deep and lasting connection with others. When we fan the sparks within us, they become irresistible beacons for the sparks in others.

Meeting Your Market Face to Face

The breathlessness of early advertising accurately reflected the enthusiasm with which the public greeted products unlike anything they'd ever imagined, much less seen before. Since then, the unchecked proliferation of consumer goods to meet every whim—and create new ones—has understandably dampened our enthusiasm for the constant stream of new product introductions. The breathless tone that once excited now just grates and irritates.

The inflated expectations most marketing efforts create are often punctured by the customer's eventual experience with the product, service, or company. Like so much else in our age, marketing has been relegated to a mostly one-way function designed to inflate a product or company image at the expense of its substance, reduced to hucksterism and the quest for the holy buck.

The most innovative customer service work being done today treats the customer, as neither the subject of study nor the object of new products or behavior, but as an active partner in developing win-win solutions. There's no more "them" when it's all "us" in this together.

Evolution of Systemic Change

While most want to grow and transform, many are afraid to try anything too new or different in marketing—even if their success was built on being new and different! Not long ago a client more or less said what many have felt: "I want things to be different as long as I don't have to change."

Resistance to change and fear, its constant companion, may not be rational, but they're real enough to short-circuit many well-intended efforts. Even small movements towards integrity, however, are powerful magnets. When values are put into action, they become a beacon to which both internal and external customers are drawn.

New paradigm proponents, however, can be trapped by the old "all or nothing" approach by insisting that systemic change must happen all at once. Paradoxically, making systemic change may only be possible step by step. Marketing with integrity can help us leverage that process. Communicating our values consciously and comprehensively through our work and workplaces can only bring us closer to our colleagues, corporations, customers, and communities. One businessman's commitment to marketing with integrity helped him address a thorny problem without requiring him to remake his organization. As Jeff Salzman, co-founder of CareerTrack, the largest producer of professional development seminars in North America, explains it, "We had a successful seminar leader who also offended many customers. I was about to fire him when I said to myself, 'Let's try to just tell the truth about him.' It worked! In a side-by-side test of brochures promoting his seminar (which teaches people to be calm and productivity under pressure), the version in which we capitalized on his unorthodox style beat the traditional approach by 42 percent!"

Salzman's creative and financially-rewarding solution acknowledged his unhappy customers without forsaking those who appreciated both the seminar and its iconoclastic leader.

By using the "problem" as a doorway to the solution, CareerTrack preserved its relationship with both one of their best seminar leaders and their customers. Highlighting the qualities that turned some customers off allowed people likely to be offended by the presenter's style to avoid his seminars. Telling the "whole" truth at the customers' decision-making stage ensured that they wouldn't feel betrayed by a promotion that omitted crucial information. Customer expectations and experience were thus brought closer together.

Birth of the New Paradigm

The promise of the new paradigm is the coexistence of industry and intimacy. This unlikely marriage is the essence of integrity. But there's no wedding possible without coequal partners. The denial of the feminine principle has left our workplaces and marketplaces spiritually and financially bankrupt. The drive for short-term profits at the expense of long-term considerations, the focus on results regardless of process, the drive to do more, better, faster has had devastating human and environmental costs.

Even in organizations, the thigh bone's connected to the hip bone; the consequence of ignoring that interconnectedness is that many organizations have become lifeless structures, skeletons stripped of all vibrancy and aliveness. The structure's been preserved, but nobody lives there anymore.

As we are increasingly challenged to change our ways or perish, we must begin to entertain questions that, even in the asking, will open us to new possibilities. If our organizations are to become members of the larger world community, our sense of responsibility must encompass stakeholders as well as stockholders. By taking the time to listen, we foster relationships that can stand the test of time. Instead of glorifying transactions at the expense of relationships, business can re-energize itself as a conduit of human connectedness.

There's an Ethiopian proverb that says, "When the heart overflows, it comes out through the mouth." By applying new principles in marketing, we can make the language of the heart the *lingua franca* of the marketplace.

Terry Mandel is the founder of a consulting firm that assists organizations in creating cultures, operations, and communications that reflect their values.

Chapter 27

Ethical Downsizing

By Michael E. Quigley

*I*n the current uncertain and tense economic climate, many organizations are compelled to "downsize." In this climate of swift and dramatic change, attention is focused on the effects of such cost-cutting measures. What is clear is that the mere act of pruning jobs does not bring immediate productivity. On the contrary, downsizing can result in declines in product quality, lost opportunities, and alienated consumers; and, it can leave survivors in the organization shaken and ineffective. More than half of the 1,468 restructured companies surveyed by the Society for Human Resource Management reported that productivity either stayed the same or deteriorated after layoffs.

The Impact of Layoff

At the heart of this dismal scenario is a consideration of corporate ethical responsibility in layoffs. One cannot underestimate the impact on an individual of the sudden loss of employment, no matter what the circumstances might be. The bewilderment people often express is like that of a homeowner who returns to find rooms ransacked, beloved objects missing—the sense of violence and invasion, the feelings of fear and loss and helplessness, descend with the same stunning force.

Often coupled with guilt, the fear and depression from feeling isolated and abandoned can bring on even worse symptoms and consequences, physical and psychological. In a culture where you are what you do, people who experience the abrupt loss of job and income feel suddenly worthless. People who personally identify most closely with their jobs and companies also suffer the worst stress when their positions are eliminated. Downsizing attacks people like an emotional buzzsaw. The belief that good job performance leads to recognition and reward by the company is shattered.

Those Left Behind

And for those employees left behind, those fortunate enough to avoid the layoff, life is often not much better. They too experience the feeling of guilt at having employment when those less fortunate, but equally capable and intelligent, have none.

After the layoff, everyone goes through the same fears for the future, anticipating that they too will fall by the next axe. Rumors fly about further cuts, and people work from day to day, becoming progressively less productive. Layoffs force everyone to take a long, hard look at their own position, for if others can be treated with such blatant calculation and disregard of human worth, then why should those who remain ever consider giving their best work, their ideas, imagination, creativity and ingenuity when they can anticipate the same treachery and callousness they have just witnessed among their peers. Better to protect themselves and seek employment elsewhere.

The argument that a business corporation exists solely for the purpose of maximizing profit for shareholders, and that managers and workers are hired strictly to achieve that end has long held sway in corporate America. As long as executives think that individuals are replaceable, they will be more or less ethically neutral, pursuing a single-minded dedication to the goal of profit. Managers are regarded strictly as "actors" on a corporate stage, morally neutral, obeying the directives of those who own the company or "machine" designed for efficiency and maximum profit. While this paradigm might serve in good economic times, it is inadequate in meeting either economic or social responsibilities of the business in times of economic hardship. One could well argue that like most individuals, the true nature of character is most vividly seen in adversity rather than in times of prosperity.

Principles of the New Paradigm

We are in need of a new model for understanding corporate responsibility vis-a-vis employees, and no utilitarian or merely pragmatic view will suffice, for neither can give adequate consideration to the concrete predicament of the individual person. Where artificial structure takes precedence over the nature of individual human beings, in which people are either manipulated without conscience or demeaned by managers compelled to act in a way which compromises their personal integrity, then I suggest there is a radical fault in the paradigm of the corporation.

If we are to learn from the hardships many experience in downsizing, I recommend that a new paradigm be built on the following five principles.

• *We need to consider the organization as a moral person* and that the organization does have responsibilities toward individuals who work within it. Conversely, equal attention needs to be given to the reciprocal responsibilities which individuals have towards the corporation.

• *Such an organization must be viewed in the fullest sense as a community,* in which each individual is accorded dignity and value. The community needs the input of the knowledge, skill, and creativity of each and every member.

• *An individual can only do this when both a covenant (as well as a contract) exists between the members of the community.* The implication of this covenant is that one is truly a member when one has real ownership (including property) of the organization, and in a limited way, control over planning the future and destiny of the organization.

• *In a true community, persons are treated as ends within themselves, as real assets, not as the means by which the ends of a distant, non-involved, board of directors are achieved.* Employees ought not to be considered as "disposable commodities" but as essential "capital" of the corporation.

• *In the structure of this business community, an individual can function creatively, providing peers with the full benefit of personal talent, knowledge, and skill.* In the language of Peter Drucker, management will be seen as an art rather than a science. Where these principles form the basis of a business community, and are expressed through mission, philosophy and effective leadership and management, a truly viable, and in the long-term, profitable organization will exist, for it possesses creative practical intelligence.

When a layoff does become unavoidable, people who are treated in a manner consistent with their human dignity leave with some sense of self-respect. In most cases today, the biggest loser in downsizing is the corporation itself, along with the shared values of loyalty and the capacity for commitment. Employees today are forced to respond to the harsh impact of restructuring by "packing their own parachute" to survive.

Devoid of true community and collegiality in the workplace, the corporation of the future faces a bleak and uncertain future in a new age of global competition. Paradoxically, only by serving the interests of its employees will it ensure its own self-interests, including its own financial viability.

Michael E. Quigley is a professor at the School of Graduate Studies at Rivier College in Nashua, New Hampshire.

Chapter 28

All's Not Fair in
Love and Work

**By Marshall Sashkin and
Richard L. Williams**

*F*or thousands of years, philosophers from Socrates on have pondered and debated the essence of fairness. And opinions still vary on what fairness is, how to explain it, and how to provide it, especially in regard to relationships at work.

We approached our study of fairness through a back door. We had observed that something was affecting bottom-line costs that was not being attended to. In an attempt to identify this "something," we simply listened to people. They said, "It isn't fair" or "That's just not fair." At first we thought that the responses had to do with equity, getting the same rewards as others for the same actions. But we quickly found that there was more there than could be explained by the equity concept. We learned that fairness is more complex, that it is multidimensional.

Ten Dimensions of Fairness

After engaging in many discussions, we identified ten specific dimensions that we feel best describe a climate of fairness.

• *Trust* is the confidence of belief that employees feel toward management. It is a binding force that helps employees overcome doubts and reduce confusion, worry, and fear.

• *Consistency* is steadiness or regularity in management action, leading to a view of management as reliable. Consistency reduces frustration because employees know what to expect, helping employees feel better prepared to meet organizational expectations.

• *Truthfulness* is fidelity in word and action on the part of management, meaning that communication is accurate and honest. When employees feel that management is truthful, they gain confidence in and respect for the organization.

• *Integrity* involves adhering to ethical precepts. Managers who behave ethically create a climate of fairness.

• *Expectations* is the clear definition and communication of duties, responsibilities, and goals. When employees have a clear understanding of what is expected of them, they are better able to achieve standards of performance.

• *Equity* involves providing equivalent rewards and sanctions for similar actions, regardless of who is involved. Each employee feels that he or she is being treated in a fair, equitable manner, that no one is getting special treatment or unfair compensation.

• *Influence* means that employees are involved in deciding how to accomplish their work goals, having real responsibility for their own results. Influence involves psychological ownership. In effect, employees become "stakeholders" in the organization, having a real "say" in terms of their contributions.

• *Justice* is the administration of rewards and sanctions that are seen as appropriate, that is, they fit the nature of the success or failure. When employees report a high degree of justice, they mean that they regard management actions as proper.

• *Respect* is the visible expression, in word and deed, of concern and regard for employees. Respect involves actions that show that employees are seen as valuable assets to the organization.

• *Procedures* that are fair require that the procedures be known to everyone and that those persons affected by the procedures participate in the application of those procedures. Fair procedures are applied to everyone in the same manner.

Measuring Fairness

Once we had defined our dimensions, we next developed a tool to assess fairness in organizations. We tried to focus on behaviors, not attitudes, hoping to identify specific managerial actions that create a climate of fairness. An example of such a behavior in each dimension follows:

Dimension Behavioral Response

Trust	I follow through and carry out my promises.
Consistency	I give the same answer, no matter who asks the question.
Truthfulness	I always say what I really mean.
Integrity	I keep my word and honor my agreements.
Expectations	I identify explicitly and communicate clearly the key expectations for jobs of all who report to me.

Equity	I take a person's contributions into account when giving praise or recognition.
Influence	I involve people in decisions that affect them directly.
Justice	I administer rewards and discipline that fit the situation.
Respect	I show by my actions that I really care about my employees.
Procedures	I make sure that everyone has a chance to use the procedures that are supposed to apply to all.

Effects of Fairness

Employees' perceptions of the climate of fairness correlate closely with such indicators as sickness and accident claim costs. We found differences unaccounted for by "wellness" or safety training programs—differences relating to how employees view the climate of fairness within the organization.

We found that managers are most concerned with issues that affect them as managers. For example, managers can't be expected to carry out their responsibilities without authority (influence); that wouldn't be fair. Nor is it fair when managers have certain performance expectations of employees, but don't let the employees know what those expectations are. Without knowing management's expectations, employees can't possibly do their jobs effectively.

Employees are more concerned with "warm and fuzzy" issues such as trust and integrity, issues that are much harder to frame in concrete terms. And yet these issues are at the heart of the "psychological contract" or the implied performance agreement between an employee and the organization. This psychological contract can be of great emotional importance to employees.

For example, most employees believe that there is an implicit agreement that if they work hard and are loyal, the organization will take care of them. When these employees are laid off or feel they have been treated unfairly, they feel betrayed and abandoned. And such feeling involve more than just dissatisfaction and the rational decision to look for a better—more fair—employer. In such circumstances, employees might even be enraged and display irrational, even vengeful responses.

When people feel this way, they are less likely to observe safety precautions. Avoidable accidents increase, and no amount of safety training will change that. Given the chance to play sick, employees may decide to see just how much they can get out of the company that wronged them—and no "wellness" program is likely to make much of a difference

Fairness does make a difference to both managers and employees. This conclusion is confirmed by our experience in training and coaching managers. We have found that issues never before broached can be raised and dealt with effectively when managers are really interested in changing. Concrete, behavioral feedback can also make a difference by engaging managers in a process of change that will contribute to employees' perceptions of management actions as truly fair.

Marshall Sashkin is Senior Associate, Office of Educational Research and Improvement, U.S. Department of Education. Richard L. Williams is Director of Training for American Stores Company in Salt Lake City, Utah.

Chapter 29

The Currency of Character

By Douglas A. Wilson

*I*n the business world, the bottom line has not changed. Profit is key to business survival. Quality brings a greater possibility of internal effectiveness and external product acceptance. Values give a clearer focus to direction and purpose. Empowerment brings greater involvement and creativity. But in the new economy, character ensures that relationships with customers, suppliers, employers, and stakeholders will be consistently profitable.

The public perception of business owners being concerned only for their own profits has not been without warrant. "Let the buyer beware" has been a legal maxim for many years. Now that stance will no longer work.

Six Shifts

I see six dimensions to the new economy.

• *First, individual customers determine the success or failure of organizations.* Governments can influence, but customers look for the best value. There is an expectation not only of price and quality, but of the social integrity of the product and its manufacturer.

• *Second, the worker has become a free agent.* Today's knowledge workers expect a place to plug in that fits them. The employer must design the position so that the work is satisfying and rewarding. The employee must serve the company, but the company must also serve the employee. In the words of Max DePree, there is an expectation of a "covenant relationship."

• *Third, partnerships and strategic alliances are the way of the future.* There are an estimated 5,000 joint ventures, large and small, between U.S. and Japanese firms. The ability to form and sustain such partnerships is critical. The expectations are ones of fair dealing and win-win relationships replacing the previous win-lose posture.

• *Fourth, capital sources are changing dramatically.* No longer is capital primarily available through banks. Executives have to establish new relationships with private sources. Going public is only one option. New capital sources such as international stock exchanges, insurance companies, pension funds, and highly tailored equity-debt offerings require new relationships that go beyond those of the traditional institutions. There is an expectation of honesty and full disclosure, of no manipulation of the up front pro forma, and of delivering what has been promised.

• *Fifth, we've gone global in our relationships.* Transnationals may design products in the U.S., manufacture in Korea, assemble in Taiwan, and sell in Brazil. Global business requires a deep understanding of different cultures and an acceptance of a common standard of right and wrong. For example, Shell has a stated policy of no bribe giving, regardless of how acceptable that may be in some countries. There is an expectation of common principles that will govern each corporate entity.

• *Sixth, we're reacting to the abandonment of once common norms of acceptable behavior.* There is a renewed interest in finding ways past the relativism produced by a pluralistic, individualistic society whose one common value seems to be that everyone should be allowed to have their own values. There is an expectation that there must be a set of common principles of what is right and wrong, principles on which we can rebuild our national character.

These six dimensions have a common denominator for success: the ability to make, keep, and manage quality relationships. Good character is fundamental to quality relationships.

What is Character?

The essence of character is how we think about and treat other people. That is why it is the currency of a new economy in which relationships take on ultimate importance.

• *Personal Character.* Individual character includes such things as integrity, promise keeping, truth telling, not taking what rightfully belongs to another, respect for other people, a desire to create harmony in relationships. It has consistency and reliability. You can count on it. It has a sense of grace, of going beyond what is expected. Thus, it always has to do with relationships between people.

Character has an "oughtness" about it. It is more than a summation of values. William Kirkpatrick clarifies the difference: "A value is essentially what you like or love to do. It is not an ought-to but a want-to." People and organizations of character act the way they do because they know this is what they should do, regardless of the circumstances that surround them.

Character is more than a reputation. Reputation is the result of how others see you. Character is defined by what you do when no one else will ever know.

- *Company Character.* Company character begins with people of character. It may become codified in policies and procedures, but it needs to be maintained by people who recognize the negative forces that are loose in the world and who keep asking the right questions. Character is never fully attained; it is always in development. But if a company aspires to greatness, its executives must work at it consistently, for there is no other way.

Creating a company of character is not easy. Well developed character in most departments won't do. The entire culture needs to be dedicated to building strong character. Character needs to be defined, developed, talked about, measured, and nurtured.

The search for company character drives us back to spiritual and moral roots: America's Judeo-Christian heritage and the philosophers of Western civilization—the book of *Proverbs* on wisdom; Cicero on friendship integrity and trust; Plato on how great leaders motivate and inspire others. How did Confucius conceive character and the virtues of both leaders and followers? Ideas from the East enrich our narrow, individualistic attitudes. They remind us of the importance of creating harmony and community as fundamental to well developed character.

All these belief systems confirm that people are what is important. If we value people, we value the people we employ. If we value people, we deliver the best product or service we can to our customers. If we value people, we are concerned for the social and physical environment in which they live. If we value people, we keep our promises; we tell the truth.

Developing and Nurturing Character

Corporate character, can be developed in ten ways:

- *Believe in the importance of character.* The cultivation of character can't be delegated. The responsibility must always stay at the top. Leadership must believe, both in head and heart, that character is the currency of the new economy—not technology, capitalization, or information, but the ability to live out truth and grace in the context of relationships. Other factors are important and necessary, but they will not lead to long-term greatness. Today more boards are establishing sub-committees on ethics and values to lay down the planks on which the organization must stand, in essence the company character. Boards are insuring that these principles are being reflected throughout the company, especially by top management.

- *Define governing principles.* Company character assumes a fundamental "way of being" that everyone agrees is worthy of aspiration. Definition begins at the top. It is shaped in the fire of dialogue over what stated principles will define this company's character—principles against which every action will be tested. It is the glue that holds all the pieces together.

- *Communicate character.* The ethics officer in one company puts ethics and values issues on e-mail on a regular basis. It educates, communicates and trains, and it has been very effective, requiring minimal time and virtually no expense.
- *Hire people of character.* Screen new hires. It is more difficult to change people than to find people who already agree with your corporate principles. Hold up your standard. Develop tools that will uncover areas of actual or potential dissonance.
- *Use 360-degree feedback.* By receiving feedback from peers, subordinates, and bosses, executives get confidential assessment on their ability to lead and manage and, most importantly, live out company values.
- *Use consultants to coach people.* Invite inside or outside consultants to observe how your teams work together, to identify gaps between what you aspire to be and where you are today, and to train people in interpersonal skills that lead to trust building and quality problem solving.
- *Review performance differently.* Performance reviews should be based not on ranking but on team goals and corporate values. While the old ranking system is still prevalent, the work of Edwards Deming encouraged its rapid replacement by a more developmental and systemic approach to development.
- *Conduct confidential interviews.* Top managers should be interviewed by a person trained in ethics and personal development and challenged to look at hard issues. Good insights are often developed as they explore tough issues without fear of reprisal.
- *Train people in new skills.* Train all employees in problem solving, conflict resolution, and interpersonal effectiveness. Motorola and Toyota are stars here. Many other companies, such as AT&T, are catching on and investing heavily to make it work.
- *Cultivate a culture that encourages constructive conflict alongside collaboration.* Intel has developed a very innovative culture by using constructive conflict, a respectful way of showing people how their ideas need to be improved. Character develops because it demands standing up for what you believe while simultaneously collaborating with others.

As character development becomes an integrating principle of business, we need to discover ways to both focus and accelerate the process. A fundamental task of the leader is to ensure that every role in the company reflects the company's character. Denial and excuses are not acceptable. Persons are measured and rewarded by high standards. The company is there to support, develop, and reward standard bearers. It is also there to coach and discipline those who do not flourish in this environment. Character then stands out as one of a company's richest assets.

Doug Wilson is president of the Wilson Consulting Group, specializing in leadership development and cultural change.

Chapter 30

Business Ethics

By Gary Edwards and Rebecca Goodell

*B*usiness ethics is constantly in the news, but the story is too often about the lack of ethics. Is it the nature of business to be constantly pressing against the limits of honest and honorable behavior? To take a profit, must business leaders take advantage?

First, let's be clear: business is not naturally unethical. Business serves the public. It creates value. It produces products and services that enrich our lives, from the homes we live in and the cars we drive to the electronic products and systems on which we rely. And business ethics is not an oxymoron. In fact, good ethics are essential to success. Most business transactions take place on a basis of trust.

We buy products expecting them to be what they purport to be and to function reliably. And when they don't, our trust erodes. If we find out that we've been cheated, our trust in that company is destroyed. And if that happens to enough of us, that company is out of business.

Business ethics is the lifeblood of a free economy. Let's cease polluting it with the kind of meanness and greed we've seen too much of lately. Let's demand better from the companies we do business with and the ones we work for. Let's rebuild the trust that makes it work!

Sometimes we talk about business as if it truly were *a jungle out there*—as if meanness, deception, and greed were necessities for survival and success.

Most leaders recognize that to succeed they must civilize the jungle by their own ethical conduct. They cite three reasons: 1) companies with good reputations attract and keep the best customers; 2) companies with good reputations attract and keep the best employees; and 3) good companies stay out of trouble. They avoid the consequences of unethical conduct and the costs that often go with it, including litigation, fines, recalls, and disruptive government intervention.

Seven Requirements

If serious misconduct is not the result of ignorance of the law, but the result of pressures to achieve unrealistic objectives, then an effective program must embrace the entire culture. We have identified seven requirements:

1. Leadership. There must be active demonstration of commitment to corporate standards in the conduct of senior executives and in the systems they deploy for planning, budgeting, forecasting, revenue recognition, and performance incentives.

2. Clear standards of conduct applicable to daily responsibilities. Many companies still rely on impenetrable codes of ethics drafted in legalese by attorneys and rendered irrelevant to key issues faced by employees on a daily basis. The prospect of compliance is enhanced by pragmatic policies addressing areas of heightened risk to misconduct such as proper ways for gathering competitive intelligence.

3. Balanced communication of company standards and business objectives. In many companies, ethics and compliance are discussed annually. Meanwhile, performance is examined quarterly, monthly, even daily. This difference is not lost on employees. In effective programs, managers strive to link discussions of performance to reminders about compliance.

4. Fair enforcement and discipline. The same rules should apply equally to all employees, including top performers and senior executives. Anything else breeds cynicism and fosters the belief that policies are made to be broken.

5. A safety valve for employees. Most "hotlines" are anything but hot. The phone just doesn't ring. Nobody wants to be a whistleblower. The best ethics and compliance offices promote "help-lines" rather than hotlines for employees who don't know the right thing to do, or who believe their manager expects them to do the wrong thing. Most employees who access the help-lines seek advice and counsel about the proper course of conduct. Such confidential assistance builds faith and trust in the office and makes it easier for employees to report misconduct.

6. Proper goal-setting and incentive and reward systems. When earnings decline or market share erodes, companies often increase sales quotas and reduce headcount without a realistic appraisal of the market or internal capacity. Companies with successful compliance efforts understand that unrealistic planning, budgeting, and forecasting create an environment where decent people may believe that top management expects them to violate company standards and the law, if necessary to succeed. The risk of bribery, theft of competitive intelligence, failure to inspect or test before shipment, substitution of inferior materials, and manipulating earnings all increase in such environments.

7. An ongoing process. Compliance is achieved only through a process of continually improving the environment in which decision making and conduct occur. Companies would do well to go beyond mere compliance programs and strive instead to understand and address the underlying causes of misconduct. In doing so, they may find that they have enhanced more than compliance.

Character Education

The first steps toward solving our problems are often very simple, but taking those steps can be painful because it means making choices. As a nation, we must make some moral choices. We have to ask ourselves: What's right? What's wrong? How do we learn the difference?

The authors of the book *The Day America Told the Truth* interviewed 5,000 people across the U.S. and found that nearly 64 percent will lie when it suits them; 74 percent will steal; and 93 percent said they alone—not the church, government, or family—determine what is moral and what is not in their lives.

Today, despite decades of increasing and expanding rights and freedoms, there is broad evidence of decline, both spiritual and material. Drugs, gangs, violence, fraud in business and the military, and the avarice of government officials are evidence of this decline.

Foremost among the many causes of this decline is the dissolution of the moral community—home, school, place of worship, and the workplace—which, for many years, shaped the character and transmitted and reinforced the values of successive generations.

It's not just that the extended family for the most part no longer exists. It's also the fact that the nuclear family increasingly has just one parent, and when it has two, both work out of economic necessity or professional choice. The influence of organized religion has waned with the secularization of society. The forces on which the country has relied to preserve and perpetuate common moral values and to prepare the character of its citizens—the family, schools, religion, and the workplace—are all less able to bear that responsibility than a generation ago.

What can we do about it? The answer must begin with each of us. Integrity means being whole, put together, being one person—the same person on the job or at home with family. One of the most seductive ideas and dangerous temptations is to believe that you can live by different rules and values in your private life than in your public or professional life.

If business people succumb to this temptation, they may behave dishonorably under pressure: they may bribe to close a deal, steal secrets from competitors to win a contract, cut costs by cutting corners, and then tell themselves that's "just the way it is" in business— "you have to do what it takes."

If business people sometimes seek to overcome professional misconduct with private virtue, politicians often try to have it the other way. They want us to judge them, not by the most recent exposure of their sordid private lives and vices. They want us to believe lust and larceny after hours have no bearing on their trustworthiness as public servants. They ask us to admire and respect their public image and forgive and forget their private shame. Most of us can't get away with such moral schizophrenia in our own lives. And we shouldn't tolerate it in business or in government.

How important should the moral failures of political leaders be when we judge their fitness for office? Most of us would agree that many indiscretions of youth can be overlooked when a candidate's adult behavior has been honorable. It's the currency and frequency of failings that reveal moral weakness. But is it fair to reject a candidate for faults we would forgive in a friend? Yes, because the judgment and conduct of leaders may affect us far more than those of a friend. And, frankly, because we want those who would lead us to be better that we are—to be stronger, smarter, wiser.

All across the world, there is a hunger for leadership, for men and women of great moral stature and conviction who are worthy of our trust and emulation.

Let's secure our own integrity by demanding of ourselves the same high standards on the job that we strive to reach at home. And let's protect our institutions by demanding integrity of those who would manage, govern, or lead us.

All heroes have their flaws, but maybe we could just begin with people who tell the truth. Let's rid ourselves of shameless liars, of spineless politicians whose opinions change with every poll, of carefully crafted public images that hide a moral vacuum. When we sweep away the debris, we may find some heroes, after all.

Gary Edwards is the president and Rebecca Goodell is a senior consultant of the Washington, D.C.-based Ethics Resource Center. They help implement codes of ethics and internal support programs and develop character education programs.

Chapter 31

In Sync Management

By Eric L. Harvey

In sync means harmony, integration, synchronized components working in unity to accomplish an objective or task. Holistic medicine refers to the interrelationship of the body, mind, and spirit. Without each of these elements being "managed" as important components of total health, system breakdown occurs.

From an environmental perspective, the viewpoint translates to "harmony with the universe." Ecological balance is nature's way of dealing with cause and effect—as evidenced by nature's often violent response to conditions that become out of kilter.

Whether the frame of reference is ecological or medical the learning is relevant and implacable: the complex systems we call organizations must be in balance.

Is Your Organization In Sync?

Today, progressive organizations are questioning their values and analyzing their beliefs. Many of these exercises are quite elaborate—involving detailed self-analysis at all levels. Typically examined are values relating to customers, stockholders, community, and employees. Such diagnosis frequently concludes with a formal articulation of philosophies and values—statements that appear in annual reports and employee handbooks and adorn offices, conference rooms, and public reception areas.

In examining hundreds of value statements over fifteen years, I've found a commonality of apparent good intentions—especially as they relate to people. Frequently stated beliefs include:
- *Our employees are our most important resource (or asset).*
- *We believe in decision making at the lowest practical level.*
- *Treat each individual with respect, trust, and dignity.*
- *We believe in fair treatment, collaboration, and partnership.*

129

While words and format vary, the essence of these messages is basically the same—*People are important to us and should be treated properly.*

Whether or not the individuals involved in developing these articles of faith and fair dealing are sincere is difficult to say. As an eternal optimist, I presume nobility of purpose. Sincerity and motives set aside, however, the harsh reality is that such value statements have meaning only when they guide actual behavior and are lived.

In syncness occurs when values and philosophies are "operationalized" via the written policies and actual practices. When what we do matches our articulated good intentions, we have balance, integration, and "fit." Far too little formal dialogue occurs concerning whether or not value-driven objectives are being translated into action. However, *in syncness* is informally evaluated every day by employees at all levels. This assessment is not being done through statistical analysis or by using specific behavioral science comparisons, but rather through simple and emotional questions, such as "Do they walk the talk" and other gut-level trigger mechanisms. The employee perspective is basic and simple—practices either match stated beliefs or they do not. It's a matter of management credibility versus hypocrisy.

In Sync Breakdowns

Incorporating the philosophies and values of the organization into its written policies and procedures is basically a simple exercise. It requires only good writers and proofreaders to ensure words like "partnership," "participation," "commitment," "respect," and "employees are our most important resource" are woven into the fabric of all key documents. Albeit a simple task, I'm continually amazed at the number of policies I find in which style and content are so antithetical to stated corporate values. The three most common offenders include: work rules, codes of conduct, complaint procedures, and discipline systems.

I recommend that you compare your organization's value statements with your actual practices in these three areas. Do you have philosophical alignment or an out of sync dilemma?

A breakdown usually occurs in the translation of policies and procedures to the behavior of our supervisors and managers. Too often, management development (training and appraisal) is conducted as if it exists in a parallel universe—with linkages to organizational values being accidental rather than by design.

To truly institutionalize stated philosophies, every educational event must be used as an opportunity to build or reinforce the individual skills and confidence necessary for value-driven management. For example, if the organization says it believes in recognizing accomplishment, supervisors and managers must develop skills in recognizing, reinforcing, and rewarding performance. If a premium is placed on improving individual performance, then the acquisition and use of coaching skills must become an integral part of the organization's training curriculum.

Finally, if the company espouses decision making at the lowest possible level, you're obligated to ensure that the requisite skills to make that happen are in place. And, when it's time for performance appraisal, each individual should be evaluated on results achieved via the application of these value-driven skills.

Incorporating values into policy language and skill-building activities are stepping stones, and yet two steps does not a journey make.

Importance of Measurement

People are more likely to do what's inspected rather than what's merely expected. What gets measured usually gets done.

In sync breakdown will occur if we fail to use the same type of measurement and evaluation in all areas. For instance, executives who adopt quality-improvement initiatives typically diagnose their current condition, set objectives, develop a system, train people, and then measure the heck out of what they do. They continually compare performance against predetermined indicators and specifications to make sure they're on track—"tweeking" the system as necessary. The irony is that while it is more pervasive and global than any single program or system, as a construct it is given far less attention and measurement.

You can—and should—measure "cultural" initiatives the same way you would look for quantifying evidence in more tangible interventions. For example, in working with a large petrochemical organization's business unit, task teams were established for the sole purpose of bringing local operational practices in sync with the company's new mission, vision, and values. One site-team developed a list of sixty-seven potential indicators that would help them determine whether or not they were "walking the talk." The exercise began with the question, "What specific behaviors will indicate that our values are being practiced?" Asking the same question will undoubtedly identify potential measurement areas and evaluation criteria.

Unless visions and values are managed with the same attention afforded to other processes, the chances of moving up the cultural continuum will be minimized. It's not only a missed opportunity, but also potentially dangerous. In fact, it might be better not to go through the exercise of articulating visions and values because without follow through, you will raise employee expectations only to be shattered in reality.

Moving Toward In Syncness

No organization can ever be totally in sync. Humans are imperfect and so, therefore, are the organizations they comprise. Like quality, *in syncness* is a journey rather than a destination. The task is to move closer rather than to arrive. You'll ensure a smoother and more productive journey by doing the following:

• *Analyze your current organizational visions and values.* Understand those that exist and create new ones as appropriate. This self-analysis is healthy and can create impressive potential for dramatic change.

• *Examine current policies and procedures* to determine their *in syncness* with articulated philosophies and values. Change those that lack obvious fit.

• *Provide supervisors, managers, and employees with training* that builds the skills and confidence to translate good intentions into specific practices. Ensure understanding that value-driven behavior is an expectation.

• *Measure and evaluate practices* against predetermined criteria to assess progress and opportunities for improvement. By paying attention, you'll demonstrate that values matter.

• *Look for every chance to "walk the talk."* Consider managing the *in sync* evaluation and adjustment process via a task team which represents diversity of work location, experience, and perception.

Managing change in complex organizations is neither simple nor expedient. The challenge is endless. *In sync* management, however, provides a clear opportunity to translate expectations into business realities. Value-driven behavior does produce results. When you walk like you talk, you get the results you want!

Eric L. Harvey is president and CEO of Performance Systems Corporation in Dallas, Texas. He developed the Positive Discipline and Peer Grievance Review Systems and co-authored the book Walk the Talk.

Chapter 32

A Perfect Ethics System for Business

By Jerry Madkins

*T*oday's headlines indicate that business executives and others are exercising poor ethical judgment. If we think of ethics as rules that help determine right and wrong thought, speech, and behavior in both private and public daily life, we must then ask, what is right and what is wrong?

A Universal Standard

Is there an ethical system whereby those making the hard business decisions can be assured they will make the right choices? I believe there is a simple ethics system which can be applied to all business actions and transactions whereby one can avoid unpleasant, unethical situations and circumstances. I call this system *Golden Rule Ethics* (GRE). GRE goes beyond the religious realm. The "Golden Rule," as it is generally known, can be stated as "Do unto others as you would have them do unto you." This exact quotation appears nowhere in religious scripture, but it is in essence the Golden Rule.

The Golden Rule appears in some form in all major world religions. These are the "Golden Rule" quotations as they appear in various religious scripture:

• *Good people proceed while considering that what is best for others is best for themselves.* (Hitopadesa, Hinduism)

• *Therefore, all things whatsoever ye would that men should do to you do ye even so to them.* (Matthew, Christianity)

• *Hurt not others with that which pains yourself.* (Udanavarga, Buddhism)

• *What you do not want done to yourself, do not do to others.* (Analects, Confucianism)

• *No one of you is a believer until he loves for his brother what he loves for himself.* (Traditions, Islam)

While GRE has a basis in all major world religions, it is based in the study of proper thought and conduct and the study of objective universal principles. GRE can be used to construct a system of moral and ethical reason for any society or culture. The question in ethics is not necessarily "who" is right or wrong, but rather "what" is right or wrong.

Golden Rule Ethics are appropriate and applicable to all groups, in all cultures, at all times. All people at all times in all cultures must bear some form of responsibility for others. That is to say we must care for one another: treat others as you want to be treated! Even the most primitive people under the most primitive circumstances realize that one cannot simply act in their own selfish interest. They know that one must be concerned about his or her fellow human beings and the group as a whole.

The major concern in developing a sound and workable business ethical system is determining what is right and wrong behavior. GRE is solely concerned with doing what is right concerning one's fellow human being based upon what a particular individual considers fair treatment for him or herself.

During the Seventh National Conference on Business Ethics, Robert C. Mercer, Chairman of the Board and Chief Executive Officer of the Goodyear Tire and Rubber Company said:

"I don't see the golden rule—the foundation of ethical behavior—in the philosophy of raiders or its results. *I see a lot of do unto others, and then sell out!* The Golden Rule—*do unto others as you would have them do unto you*—may disappear from the business world if corporations and business people don't begin living and working at it."

Ethical Perversions

GRE can and should work in the business environment. The reason for its not working is that it is not being applied as it should, or it is being ignored altogether. Many have opted for the concept, *"Do unto others before they do unto you."* This relegates a businessman to the level of believing that because everyone else is doing something, then it might be right for all. The GRE concept quickly obliterates the belief that it is appropriate to bend the rules.

Alasdair MacIntyre, a contemporary philosopher, has said, "Today's approach to morality has degenerated into modern emotivism (where) every moral statement is no more than an expression of one's own feelings or emotions." In emotivism, one does what one *feels* is right. Therefore, if greed feels right, one would engage in it. If insider trading feels right, then one should engage in it. If breaking into the opponents' headquarters feels right, then one should do it. If begging millions of dollars in the name of religion and then living a luxurious lifestyle off the proceeds of the people on fixed incomes feels right, then do it. We can become cynical and believe whatever feels right is the right thing to do because everyone else seems to be doing it.

To counter this trend, business schools are adding, revising, and implementing courses in ethics. This is a very good measure, but new courses in ethics are not the total answer. GRE is the answer. There is no course which can really teach us right and wrong behavior. The way one acts and thinks has been developing long before we take a course at the university. Likewise, ethical conduct that is to guide one through life is well set before we assimilate a company's ethical code of conduct.

Ethics covered in colleges and codes of ethics in companies can only supplement an internal system of good ethical reasoning. Haven C. Bunke, editor of *Business Horizons,* says: "Codes of ethics seem pale and toothless. Can we change in a few classrooms what students have learned in real life situations over the years? What do we have to say that students wouldn't better learn by reading Plato's *Crito,* St. Augustine's *Confessionis,* Shakespeare's *Anthony and Cleopatra?"*

Paul O. Sand, Executive Director of National Conference of Christians and Jews says, "In my judgment, ethics cannot be *taught.* Rather, ethics are *caught* and developed over time and affected by human relationships and life experiences."

I concur. Effective ethical behavior is not taught but "caught" and properly used in the concept of GRE. No matter what level of moral development one may have reached, it is relatively easy to decide what is right or wrong by using GRE. For example:

• *Would you want to be denied a job because of your color, race, national origin, or religious preference? The answer is no; therefore, do not do this to others in your business dealings.*

• *Would you want your well established portfolio to be devastated or possibly destroyed because some broker practices insider trading? The answer is no; therefore, do not do this to others in your business dealings.*

• *Would you want your daughter's, wife's, or sister's next job or promotion to be dependent on whether she submitted favorably to her supervisor's sexual advances? The answer is no; therefore, do not do this to others in your business dealings.*

• *Would you want fellow office workers to withhold vital information from you that could prevent you from receiving your next merit pay raise? The answer is no; so do not do this to others in your business dealings.*

The GRE concept can easily come to life in one's ethical reasoning without violating other philosophical ground rules. You simply treat people as you would want to be treated yourself.

There are two major problems with GRE when applied to business. First, GRE may fail to give a certain business the "Competitive

Edge." The old saying, "nice guys finish last" can apply in GRE. While you are trying to do the right thing in your business, your competition exploits your "nice guy approach." This could ruin or bankrupt your organization. Secondly, and perhaps more crucially, GRE is not a short-term solution; it works in the long run. Other business personnel and the general public may simply not believe that a business really wants to treat its employees, competitors, and customers fairly. GRE will most likely be viewed as a cheap advertising gimmick.

GRE is easy to understand and apply to all business situations. Senior executives who agree with GRE should insist upon adherence to this concept, even if immediate benefits are not readily realized. GRE always will work!

Jerry B. Madkins is an assistant professor of management at Tarleton State University in Stephenville, Texas.

Chapter 33

From Ethics to Integrity

By Randy Pennington

*I*n the best of all worlds, ethical behavior would be the expected way of doing business. Employees would make decisions based on the personal commitment to honesty, integrity, and fairness. They would carry out their duties, promote the organization's ideals, and maintain the trust of their customers, suppliers, co-workers, and communities. In this perfect world, no one would succumb to temptation and the lure of expedience. Unfortunately, there is no perfect world.

We live in a world where trust has deteriorated into widespread cynicism. The increased demands of a highly competitive market have forced us to consider short cuts once dismissed as unthinkable. Scandals and improprieties (real or imagined) reinforce the belief that playing by the Golden Rule is now passé. Bedfellows abound at a time when true partnerships are needed to meet the challenges of building strong relationships.

Written Codes Are Not Enough

Written ethics codes and value statements are the traditional response to the challenge of unifying the organization's beliefs and behavior. They are intended to provide direction and ensure consistency of expectation and performance. They have worked in many cases. In others, written ethics codes have been routinely ignored while behavior that is, at best, questionable becomes the order of the day.

Written codes and value statements are necessary, but they do not ensure integrity in word and deed. They are merely the first step in a long and difficult process that moves the organization from ethics compliance toward a commitment to integrity in products, services, and relationships. Only then will the inspiring values statements that hang on the wall be transformed into performance that promotes trust, mutual respect, and commitment to doing what is right.

Behavior that destroys organizational integrity is more likely to occur when these five factors have greater impact than written codes and value statements:

1. The culture makes it okay. Adlai Stevenson said, "Laws are never as effective as habits." Most people know, for example, that the law dictates the speed limit. Yet, many routinely exceed it based on habit. An organization's culture is demonstrated by its habits. Overlooking or even rewarding questionable behavior sends the message that it is condoned or even encouraged. A study done by John Delaney and Donna Sockell at Columbia University reported that 40 percent of respondents who chose to act unethically were rewarded, either explicitly or implicitly. Determine the habits that send messages about the importance of rules and standards, and you will discover the aspects of the organization's culture that influence integrity.

2. Systems reinforce behavior. Systems are the tools to promote efficiency and consistency. They are powerful vehicles for developing habits though repetitious performance. Effectively designed systems in areas such as compensation, performance management, and purchasing are important components of an environment that has grown beyond compliance to ethics and embraced integrity as a way of life. Otherwise, systems can unconsciously promote behavior that contradicts the organization's good intentions.

3. Pressure to achieve results with limited resources. It is a challenge to maintain or increase productivity levels in times of decreasing resources. Leaders may be tempted to say, "Get it done any way you can." There is, however, an inherent danger in this message. Employees respond by cutting corners, and potentially open the door to actions that destroy trust and credibility. Directives must communicate the expectation of results and responsibility for how they are achieved.

4. People blindly follow the directions and example of others. There are two situations where this could occur. The first is when an inspiring, charismatic leader persuades others to follow his or her direction regardless of the consequences. There are numerous examples of well meaning individuals whose judgment was clouded by the ability of a great motivator.

The second is when employees assume that the directives they receive from management should be followed without question. The assumption is that all decisions have been examined before they are implemented. The solution to blind compliance in both scenarios is educated employees who understand the organization's mission and values, think for themselves, and are willing to ask questions when they arise.

5. The lure of expedience. Ben Franklin wrote that success is primarily a function of what you are and that one must master 13 internal principles to be achieve it. External trappings were the result rather than a primary indicator. That view has changed.

Our culture sends powerful messages that say success is based on what you have. The ends justify the means. The desire to have it all today can lead to short-term thinking, rationalizing actions, and cutting corners.

Making the Move from Ethics to Integrity

Kathleen Purdy, writing in *Ethical Management,* says, "What started out in many organizations as mere (ethics) compliance is now a very powerful process—one that weaves together many other programs aimed at change." Leaders are discovering that successful products, services, and relationships are all connected by a common thread—integrity. It goes beyond ethics, Total Quality Management, customer service, and empowerment to build trust and commitment among customers, employees, suppliers, and the community. The following ideas will help your organization make the transition:

• *Begin where your influence is highest.* Dr. Stanley Pearle, founder of Pearle Vision, is fond of saying, "The customer is smarter than you think. You must deliver what you promise. That is the only way to develop trust." Lasting change is an inside-out process. Individuals must change before organizations can change. A foundation of trust, mutual respect, and commitment must exist internally with employees and suppliers before moving externally to customers and communities.

• *State expectations, but avoid a new "Integrity Program."* The goal is to make integrity the guiding principle for products, services, and relationships. New programs become the latest example of MBBS—Management By Best Seller. Instead, state your expectations in an open, honest manner so that employees understand their obligation to customers, suppliers, communities and each other. Explain that strategic initiatives such as empowerment, self-managed teams, new performance management practices, and ethics codes are simply the tools to help the organization meet those obligations. Avoid any hype, admit you are constantly working to fine-tune your own performance, and ask everyone to join you in the goal of making integrity the number one operating principle. Continuously remind everyone that the ultimate goal is on-going trust, loyalty, and commitment of customers, employees, suppliers, and communities in a way that insures everyone's long-term viability and survival.

• *Design systems and structures that promote integrity, trust, mutual respect, and commitment.* Systems and structures create habits in organizations. Each system should be judged by the following three criteria: Are we doing what we said we would do? Are we providing what we said we would provide? Does the system reinforce our commitment to integrity, trust, and mutual respect. Organizational systems, both internal and external, send a message about our integrity that is more powerful than any ethics code or values statement.

• *Hold people accountable for achieving results in ways that promote integrity of products, services, and relationships.* Leaders must reinforce that there is no "either/or" alternative. Results must be achieved through actions that demonstrate integrity in products, services, and relationships. This message is sent through promotions, compensation, perks, and handling performance that does not meet their expectations.

• *Educate to provide knowledge and skills then empower people to act.* The goal of ethics codes is often compliance with stated requirements. Focusing on integrity can empower every individual to recognize, confront, and correct performance that diminishes trust in products, services, and relationships. Individuals and teams should spend time discussing and understanding the impact of decisions and actions to acquire the knowledge to improve in the future. Skill building provides the tools that enable them to respond effectively when situations arise.

The number one characteristic people want from their leaders is integrity. We tend to trust leaders who walk their talk on a personal level. It is a crucial ingredient, but it is only the first step in a long process. Ultimately, leaders must become passionate in their zeal to move toward a better world that expects, encourages, and promotes integrity in products, services, and relationships.

Randy Pennington is president of Pennington Performance Group, Dallas, Texas. He is co-author of On My Honor, I Will: Leading with Integrity in Changing Times.

Chapter 34

Shaping Values

By Tom Peters

*T*he executive who learns to give clear signals and to cope with fragmented working days and messy agendas can better shape the values and events of an organization and leave a mark of excellence on his or her company.

My concept of the top management task fits the disorderly facts of life. It considers the effective executive as a communicator, persuader, and above all a consummate opportunist—adept at taking advantage of each item in the random succession of time and issue fragments that crowd his or her day.

In an untidy world, where goal setting, option selection, and policy implementation hopelessly fuze together, the shaping of robust institutional values through a principle of ad hoc opportunism becomes preeminently the mission of the chief executive and most of the senior colleagues.

The nature of this value-shaping process is not obvious. The art of value management blends strategic foresight with a shrewd sense of timing and the political acumen necessary to build stable, workable coalitions. Fortunately, the practical exercise of these skills is actually enhanced by the untidiness of typical executive choice processes.

Top management's actions over time constitute the guiding, directing, and signaling process that shapes values in the near chaos of day-to-day operations. Top management is at the apex of the symbolic signaling system, not the hard product delivery system. Because senior managers cannot act directly or promptly to resolve issues, their daily efforts must focus on sending effective and appropriate signals.

Executives who see their role in these terms are aware that symbolic management is a course of unparalleled opportunity and risk. Knowing that subordinates will eventually make detailed interpretations of every activity, they will be scrupulously careful to avoid distracting signals.

Beyond that, they need to be able to articulate their vision in a compelling way. If it is in shaping values that senior executives can most efficiently use their time, it is symbols that are their primary value-shaping tools As educators, they have quite an arsenal of pedagogical tricks at their disposal:

• *Manipulation of settings,* including the creation of forums and rules of debate designed to focus on critical concerns;

• *Careful use of language,* including insistently asked questions;

• *Consistent and frequent feedback and reinforcement,* including the careful and selective interpretation of past results to stress a chosen theme;

• *Shifts of agenda and time allocation* to signal a change in priorities;

• *Selective seeding of ideas* among various internal power groups, and cultivation of those that win support.

Collectively, these enable the CEO to intervene purposefully and effectively in what one philosopher called "the brute flow of random detail that adds up to everyday experience."

Thirteen Observations

The heightened awareness of ethics has spawned an industry of mindless, "do good, be good" writings. But dealing with ethics isn't so easy. The point was driven home after I accepted an invitation to speak about ethics. I spent many a restless night grappling with the easy simplifications that ignore messy reality.

This set of somewhat disjointed observations is one byproduct.

• *Ethics is not principally about headline issues*—responding to the Tylenol poisoning or handling insider information. Ethical concerns surround us all the time, on parade whenever we deal with people in the course of the average day. How we work out the "little stuff" will determine our response, if called upon, to a Tylenol-size crisis. When disaster strikes, it's far too late to seek out ethical touchstones.

• *High ethical standards*—business or otherwise—are, above all, about treating people decently. To me (as a person, businessperson, and business owner) that means respect for a person's privacy, dignity, opinions, and natural desire to grow; and people's respect for (and by) coworkers.

• *Diversity must be honored.* To be sure, it is important to be clear about your own compass heading; but don't ever forget that other people have profoundly different—and equally decent—ethical guidance mechanisms.

• *People, even the saints, are egocentric and selfish.* We were designed "wrong" in part from the start. Any ethical framework in action had best take into account the troublesome but immutable fact of our inherently flawed character.

- *By their very nature, organizations run roughshod over people.* Organizations produce powerlessness and humiliation for most participants with more skill than they produce widgets.
- *Though all men and women are created equal, some surely have more power than others.* Thus, a central ethical issue in the workplace (and beyond) is the protection of and support for the unempowered—especially the front-line worker and the customer.
- *While one can point to ethically superior (and profitable) firms, such as Herman Miller, most of us will spend most of our working life in compromised—i.e., politicized—organizations.* Dealing with office politics is a perpetual ethical morass. A "pure" ethical stance in the face of most firms' political behavior will lead you out the door in short order, with only the convent, monastery, or ashram as alternatives. The line between ethical purity and arrogant egocentricism (i.e., a holier-than-thou stance toward the tumult of everyday life) is a fine one.
- *Though I sing the praises of an "action bias," ethical behavior demands that we tread somewhat softly in all of our affairs.* Unintended consequences and the secondary and tertiary effects of most actions and policies far outnumber intended and first-order effects. I sometimes think—as a manager, as a "change agent"—that dropping out is the only decent, ethical path; our best-intended plans so often cause more harm than good. (Think about it: leaving the world no worse off than when you arrived is no mean feat.)
- *The pursuit of high ethical standards in business might well be served by the elimination of many business schools.* The implicit thrust of most MBA programs is that great systems and great techniques win out over great people.
- *Can we live up to the spirit of the Bill of Rights in our work places?* Can "good business ethics" and "good real-life ethics"—and profit—coincide on a routine basis? One would hope that the answer is yes, although respect for the individual has hardly been the cornerstone of American industry's traditional approach to its work force.
- *Capitalism and democracy in society are messy.* But I believe that they have far fewer downsides and far more upsides than any alternative so far concocted. The same can be said for capitalism and democracy inside the firm—e.g., wholesale participation or widespread ownership.
- *Great novels, not management books, might help.* There are no easy answers, but there are fertile fields for gathering ideas. If you wish to be appropriately humbled about life and relationships and the possibility of ethical behavior, read Dostoyevsky, Forster or Garcia Marquez instead of Drucker, Blanchard or Peters. Then reconsider your latest magisterial proclamation.

• *Each of us is ultimately lonely.* In the end, it's up to each of us and each of us alone to figure out who we are, who we are not, and to act more or less consistently on those conclusions.

A Good Start

In my view, anyone who is not very confused all the time about ethical issues is out of touch with the frightful (and joyous) richness of the world. But at least being actively confused means that we are actively considering our ethical stance and that of the institutions we associate with. That's a good start.

Tom Peters is chairman of The Tom Peters Group, in Palo Alto, California. He is the co-author of the bestsellers In Search of Excellence *and* A Passion for Excellence *and author of* Thriving on Chaos.

Chapter 35

Return to Basic Beliefs and Priorities

By Francis G. "Buck" Rodgers

*F*or leaders, one of the most critical jobs is setting priorities: narrowing tasks so the organization knows what's required. This means having a very clear set of goals, objectives, and measurements. What's lacking in American business today are goals that can be transformed into specific measurements for each individual.

The trouble begins when you emphasize a myriad of things and nobody knows whether to spend more hours writing a proposal, calling on prospects, or servicing existing customers. It's the allocation of time and resources for everything you do that counts. The key is in the structure and discipline each person brings to his or her work.

Whether you are an entrepreneur or part of an established company, you must imbue the entire organization with your beliefs, vision, and priorities. Beliefs and innovation come from getting people together and brainstorming. Beliefs should epitomize the way you want to do business. That's the umbrella under which everything stands. So many established companies and start-up businesses don't bother to convey what they're really trying to do. They don't convey principles or beliefs.

Establish a set of principles that fosters free thinking. Turn your goals into specific objectives. From there, it is important to take periodic checks to see if these goals are being achieved. Many people set objectives, but few sit down to a day of reckoning. In this inspection process it's critical for management to say more than "I'm here to inspect." He or she needs to say, "I'm here to help. Let's try to understand the problem." And to ask, "Am I contributing to it?" Maybe there's something else needed in the business, such as more training or more education, or maybe the manager isn't providing the best guidance.

Mutually agree on a course of action. Once, a young manager asked me how to tell someone he is not doing his job. I said that's exactly what you do—you tell him. The hardest thing for most managers is telling someone he's not performing well. But you owe it to people to be honest. You need to determine if it's a personal problem or a business problem. You ask the why, not just dictate. Anybody can be autocratic. But you don't get much done that way, through fear. A good manager leads through his or her own honesty and integrity.

Look at your business tactics and strategies. This has a lot to do with the prime thing I ask people—do you have the right set of talent in your organization? Is there a discipline to your recruiting? Personally, I wouldn't let anyone in personnel hire my people. That's the line manager's job. If you're going to hold people accountable for results, then give them the freedom to choose whom they want.

Train your line management to make the selection and to recognize those who do the best job. If you've got good talent and bench strength, then look at your education and training, and not just entry-level but continuing education. What are you doing to keep people at a high level of knowledge? Not surprisingly, that's where companies shortchange themselves.

If you provide the right environment and give people a chance to excel, you can achieve any goal. So there is nothing really sophisticated or revolutionary about leadership or good management. It means doing some very fundamental, commonsense things—and doing them well. It's doing 1,000 things 1 percent better, not 1 thing 1,000 percent better. Once in a while you get a big hit. But to me, it's a world of inches. You move to a higher level of excellence. Then you attempt to go further, to another level, by trying something new. You keep inching up and reaching for your utopia. But in reality, most of us don't find utopia. We just work toward it.

So if you establish beliefs and principles, set clear objectives with the right priorities—and give people the chance to excel—you can achieve any goal. Above all, what is required is living up to the word integrity. People can count on what you say as well as what you do. You meet your commitments. Ultimately, it comes down to you and me—the most valuable resources of any well-run organization.

Francis G. "Buck" Rodgers is known throughout the business world as a motivator, articulator of ideas, and practitioner of excellence. He is the author of Getting the Best Out of Yourself and Others.

Chapter 36

Climate Control

By Hyrum W. Smith

Years ago five women filed lawsuits against Stroh Brewing Co. in Minneapolis for sexual harassment. Their complaint was this: "The company's advertising creates a climate in which sexual harassment is more easily tolerated."

If a company wants an atmosphere of equality in the workplace, it will need to focus on corporate "climate control." Just as one kind of climate determines whether it is possible to grow sugar cane and pineapples in Hawaii (and that it is not possible to grow these same things in the Russian tundra), so does a corporate climate determine whether we create equality, trust and self-reliance at the office, or inequality, distrust, and dependency.

By definition, *climate* refers to the "prevailing influences or environmental conditions characterizing a place, group, or period." Temperature, wind velocity, and precipitation are the elements farmers look at to determine what crops are likely to grow in a given climate. Among the prevailing influences and environmental conditions a CEO needs to examine are language, tone and intent. These elements foster one type of climate or another.

Individual perceptions—or the Belief Windows of those who are employed in a given area—establish the climate in a corporate setting. The beliefs of the people drive the behavior of the believers and ultimately create their reality. We attempt to describe our realities with language, and this verbalized reality then creates the conditions or quandaries of various corporate climates.

In the book *People in Quandaries,* which my father used as the textbook for the university-level General Semantics class he taught, Wendell Johnson compares these quandaries to verbal cocoons. He states:

> *Quandaries are like verbal cocoons in which individuals elaborately encase themselves, and from which they do not tend to hatch. The peculiar structure of these cocoons appears to be determined in great measure by the structure of the society in which they are formed—and the structure of this society has been and continues to be determined significantly by the structure of the language which we so unconsciously acquire and unreflectively employ.*

We need to become conscious and reflective about what is on our Belief Windows and about the language we use that keeps those beliefs there. None other than Ben Franklin suggested a process for becoming conscious. In *A Letter from Father Abraham* (1758), he writes:

> *I recommend to you, that in order to obtain a clear sight and constant sense of your errors, you would set apart a portion of every day for the purpose of self-examination. For the acquirement of solid, uniform, steady virtue, nothing contributes more, than a daily strict self-examination, by the lights of reason, conscience, and the word of God; joined with firm resolutions of amending what you find amiss, and fervent prayer for grace and strength to execute those resolutions. This method is very ancient and practiced since in every age, with success, by men of all religions.*

It is not sufficient that you make use of self-examination alone; therefore, I also instruct you in the prudent and deliberate choice of some disinterested friend to remind you of such misconduct as must necessarily escape your severest inquiry. Every prudent man ought to be jealous and fearful of himself, lest he run away too hastily with a likelihood instead of truth; and abound too much in his own understanding. It is necessary that you should have a monitor. Most men are very indifferent judges of themselves and often think they do well when they sin; and imagine they commit only small errors, when they are guilty of crimes.

First, become aware and reflective about reality. What does it take to change a corporate climate (individual belief windows)? It requires, first, that a significant mass within the group become aware and reflective about what is going on. It means they become willing to read their own patterns and confront the beliefs driving their behavior. It also means getting clear on what the patterns mean which produce their behaviors—or, in other words, it requires that we tell ourselves the truth about our real intent. If it is true that "out of the abundance of the heart the mouth speaketh"—and I believe this is true—it means examining how we are in our hearts.

Anne Wilson-Schaef, author of *When Society Becomes an Addict*, suggests those in the less powerful levels of a group hierarchy are likely to be very accurate in discerning both their own patterns and those of upper management's. In order to survive, even short term, they are required to deal with the climates which these patterns produce. Upper management, for instance, does not have to deal with the climates of the less powerful people in their company—not for short-term survival. They can park in designated parking places, go straight to the executive offices, hire an administrative assistant to keep at bay anyone they don't care to deal with, and, in short, establish almost total climate control. And they can choose to believe that how they say things are, is how things are. They can encase themselves in a cocoon.

Second, choose a process for identifying your personal governing values, then act from this root system. In light of Franklin's advice, however, it makes sense to invite feedback on issues from throughout the company—from people who are affected by an issue. This can come in the form of advisory councils, Quality Circles, outside research studies, individual interviews, and a variety of other methods. What will be important is that the effort be known for being a genuine effort, rather than a token, and that the real intent is to attend to the needs of those involved.

Here at FranklinCovey, we provided an eight-week women's seminar which has grown into a task force that is now providing us with feedback on how we are really doing in the area of equality. I'm not suggesting this is comfortable. But we teach people, in our time management seminar, to endure short-term discomfort for long-term well-being; we believe we need to practice what we teach.

Reasons for upper management to choose to acknowledge and address the beliefs of their workers are many. I believe the reason behind management's choice to address inequality and gender harassment is the key factor in creating a climate of equality. For instance, just from a pragmatic stance, a CEO could decide it would, over time, be good for the bottom line to address harassment issues. Or from a legal standpoint a company could say, "We've covered ourselves; we've offered such and such training and we established this or that task force. We aren't liable."

Our employees will read the patterns, identify the beliefs and principles which are the explanation for the patterns they see, and they will know whether upper management has attended—once again—to themselves and their own system, or if, in fact, they have attended to and served their employees. For the latter to occur, the reason prompting a genuine look at issues of equality and gender harassment would need to derive from basic governing values of the corporate leaders.

The dissatisfaction we see in the workplace is not with the corporate governing values; it is where the individual governing values of the leaders are at odds with stated corporate values. The resulting dissonance affects the Belief Windows of the employees so that what gets written there is:

"I don't care what the policy says; you can't do such and such."

"They'll never listen."

"Nothing will be done about it. Why bother saying anything?"

And thus a climate is established that feels unequal, unfair, and over time, becomes unfruitful.

Unless one's own ox has been gored, there is no *urgent* need to address the issue—unless there is a vital personal governing value which would cause a person to extend himself for his own or for another's well-being and spiritual growth. So what is the answer to gender harassment and discrimination? It is for us to discover the truth about what we are doing. We do this by becoming conscious and by reflecting on what we are doing and where we are coming from. We are helped in becoming conscious by inviting feedback from disinterested, trusted sources who will advise us of what they see.

Finally, climate is the critical factor in the long-term success and staying power of a business. Customers feel the climate in which a company operates; employees feel it; and it doesn't take them long to figure it out. Climate is more important, long-term, than what a business does—and I am not denigrating the importance of what we do. I am suggesting that what we do may never be enough if we have not attended to how we are—which is what climate is all about.

Hyrum W. Smith is co-chairman of FranklinCovey Company in Salt Lake City, Utah.

Who Is Ethical?
Where Are Ethics Practiced?

Chapter 37

The Ethics of Partnerships

By Wolfgang R. Schmitt

*A*t Rubbermaid, we believe that ethical and creative partnerships with our consumers, customers, suppliers, communities, shareholders, and associates will enable us to improve the value we create to delight our partners.

To me, *value* is the key word. We excel together when we make consumers happy, and we make them happy by delighting them with our value. And *value* must be interpreted using a value pyramid consisting of dual price, service, timeliness, and innovation.

Consumers have a limitless appetite for greater value. If we together can improve value and delight our customers, we grow together. Real growth and improvement are the primary sources of wealth, and wealth creation need not be a zero-sum game.

What makes free enterprise so unique, so successful, and so widely embraced around the globe, is that an individual can acquire wealth in ways that do not harm others, but actually benefit them.

We believe that the only way to consistently create wealth is by satisfying the material needs of others (delighting customers). Profits reward all of us for successfully fulfilling the legitimate expectations of our business partners. This belief makes money-making ethical.

Trust Plays a Key Role

Only through consistent ethical behavior can we establish the trust which allows genuine business partnerships to form and to grow. Trust has the lead role in reducing the unpredictability of mutual behavior as commitments made are honored. Trust facilitates dealing with unforeseen events in a mutually acceptable manner. And trust economizes the cost of bargaining, monitoring, and settling disputes. A healthy, trusting partnership allows us to meet the ever-higher value expectations of our consumers—the duality, price, service, timeliness, and innovation equation.

We see three types and levels of trust:

• *Mutual or contractual trust*—each partner adheres to written or oral agreements.

• *Competence trust*—partners expect and act on the premise that the trading partner will perform its role competently.

• *Goodwill trust*—the mutual expectation and commitment of being responsive to requests from your partner. Both partners respond to any possible opportunity to improve value. To prove themselves worthy of goodwill trust, partners must be ethical in all transactions and take initiatives to continuously improve value while refraining from taking unfair advantage. Goodwill trust behavior consists of actions that increase one's vulnerability to another whose behavior is not necessarily under one's control.

When ethical behavior is present in all three types of trust in your partner relationships, you can best improve value continuously. In fact, I submit that the governing rule of thumb for ethical partnerships is this: Does any given action create better value for our mutual consumers?

Two Major Theories

Let's look at two major theories in moral philosophy: deontological and teleological theories.

As Hunt and Vitell describe in *A General Theory of Marketing Ethics:* Deontologists believe that "certain features of the act itself, other than the value it brings into existence" makes an action or rule right. A prime example of this approach is the *Golden Rule* attitude, or the "Do unto others as you would have them do unto you."

Teleologists, on the other hand, "believe that there is one and only one basic or ultimate right-making characteristic, based upon the consequences of the decision." In other words, it is "the comparative value of what is, probably will be, or is intended to be brought into being." Teleologists propose that we would determine the consequences of various behaviors in a situation and evaluate the goodness or badness of all the consequences. Our behavior then is "ethical" if it produces a greater balance of short- and long-term good-over-evil than any available alternative.

Successful business partners engage in both deontological and teleological evaluations in making ethical judgment calls.

Practical Standards

Because we live in a constantly changing world and must continuously deal with new people in new places, simply using prescriptive ethical input won't allow us to deal successfully with the many complex ethical issues. We also need more descriptive ethical inputs from the industry and organization and from personal experiences—to see the ethical problem, to develop creative alternatives, to assess the consequences, and to make the best ethical decision to achieve a win-win resolution with our partners.

Today, people are more secular in their everyday lives and decisions. Many people, given the opportunity, are not much dissuaded by spiritual values and motives from secularism, materialism, hedonism, and greed. And so we need to reorder our priorities and develop more powerful justifications for ethical behavior for our organizations in a secular world.

The carrot of heaven and the stick of hell must be replaced or supplemented with rewards and consequences which can be brought to bear here and now. Leaders must clearly identify the rewards and consequences and communicate them broadly.

To create an ethical partnership, partners must achieve three things: 1) *clarity*—what do we expect from one another? 2) *equity*—what's in it for each of us? and 3) *justice*—where do we go to resolve ethical issues? The leaders must believe that good ethics is good business, set the moral tone, lead by personal example, abandon the language of coercion—"Do this or else"—and develop a language of choice, "Let's try this."

Successful ethical partnerships find ethically-driven compromises, not power-driven compromises. They reward and reinforce good behavior, define consequences for bad behavior, deal globally at both the macro and micro ethical levels.

I would advise you to select your business partners very carefully. Simplify your relationships with candor. Trust but verify that both partners are meeting their commitments. Demand fairness from your own organization and your partners.

Create, train, reward, and reinforce partner teams. Balance the drive for profit with both a short- and a long-term view. Review your compensation system to be sure it supports your ethical partnership philosophy and strategies. Maintain confidentiality on one another's proprietary information. Share the risks, share the problems, and share the rewards with your partners.

Remember, even a negative result, when dealt with properly, can strengthen the partnership. Genuine business partnerships result in a healthy interdependence where the walls that separate two organizations are either eliminated or dramatically reduced.

Negotiating Differences

The most difficult part of partnering is negotiating and resolving the inevitable differences between partners. Rather than adversarial or arms-length negotiations, I highly favor the approach of principled negotiations. Principled negotiations can occur only where there is trust, candor, and forthrightness in a relationship, where both partners will spell out their musts and their wants so that a true win-win alternative can be developed.

Principled negotiation is much like negotiating with jujitsu. Rather than resisting the force of the other side, you conspire to use your skill to channel your energies into exploring interests and inventing options for mutual gain.

The rules of principled negotiation are straightforward: *Don't bargain over positions; separate people and personalities from the problem; focus on interests, not positions; invent options for mutual gains; insist on using objective, agreed-to criteria; and know your best alternative to a negotiated agreement if your ethics are about to be trashed by a powerful, yet unscrupulous, partner.*

When we follow the rules of principled negotiations, we can be successful in both the short as well as long term. We, like historical economists, know that trust resulting from ethical partnerships is crucial to achieving competitiveness and industry leadership. Much of the economic backwardness and failure in the world can be explained by the lack of ethics leading to a lack of trust. Achieving ethical, win-win partnerships is a continuing journey—one only we can lead.

Wolfgang R. Schmitt is chairman of the board and CEO of Rubbermaid Incorporated.

Chapter 38

The Ethic of Environmentalism

By Edgar S. Woolard

*L*ooking ahead to the next decade and beyond, I see one of our chief concerns will be environmental stewardship. An unexpected turn of events in this arena—be it an accident or the cumulative effect of regulatory or policy development—could derail our progress toward the vision of the kind of nation or corporation we want to be in the next century.

The challenge to companies like Du Pont is that our continued existence as a leading manufacturer requires that we excel in environmental performance and that we enjoy the non-objection—indeed, even the support—of the people and governments in the societies where we operate.

What's at stake is the ability of our manufacturing industry to continue to serve well the growing needs of society. Clearly, industry has to participate in the political process to oppose poor policies and support well-crafted initiative, including bills that encourage waste minimization and recycling. And while we may not agree on many points, industry and environmental groups need ongoing dialogue. Business and industry will always have a moral and economic responsibility to assist the public in understanding risk/benefit issues.

Environmentalism is now a mode of operation for every sector of society. We have to develop a stronger identity of ourselves as environmentalists. As Du Pont's chief executive, I'm also Du Pont's chief environmentalist.

I'm calling for corporate environmentalism—which I define as an attitude and a performance commitment that place corporate environmental stewardship fully in line with public desires and expectations.

Five Common Obstacles

What historically has stood in the way of corporate environmentalism? I see five obstacles.

• *Corporate insensitivity to public opinion.* For a long time, there was a perception in industry that environmentalism was out of step with the mainstream of society. Many executives saw environmentalism as a nuisance and environmentalists as radicals. But the most powerful environmentalist group in every modern society is now the general public. People have declared in opinion polls and in elections that the environment will be protected. Environmentalism is the mainstream.

• *Industry's lack of environmental credibility.* How do we build credibility? Credibility is directly tied to performance. We must adopt even greater safeguards to avoid incidents. When problems occur, we must swiftly and effectively respond. Communication is critical to the success we will have in dealing with environmental problems. But communication is only beneficial if we back up what we say with concrete action.

• *The technocracy of modern industrial corporations.* Science and technology are marvelous things. At Du Pont, we have witnessed the many good things that science and engineering make possible. However, we sometimes position ourselves on an environmental issue on the basis of available technical or scientific data alone.

We have been too inclined to act as though public wishes and concerns matter less than the technical opinions of scientists and engineers. But public opinion must be dealt with regardless of the technical facts.

I don't mean to say that industry should roll over and play dead every time someone makes a protest. Economic decisions should not be made on the basis of an alarmed public's reaction to overstated news stories. But neither can decisions be made solely on the technical merits. There is a point at which every company should have the good sense to know whether persisting with a particular position is in the best interest of society at large, whatever the technical merits of the argument. To develop the understanding of when that point is reached will require a new corporate sensitivity to public concerns, and an opening of new channels of communication with the public.

• *Corporate attitudes.* We will also have to change some corporate attitudes. For example, the truly farsighted manager will not spend just what is necessary to meet minimum technical requirements of the law. Where reasonable improvements can be identified that will bring long-term environmental benefits and enhance public acceptance, we must have the vision to implement such changes—even at cost penalties beyond mere compliance.

For instance, Du Pont used to dispose of inert wastes from one of our manufacturing sites into the Atlantic Ocean off the coast of New Jersey. Some time ago, our government permit to continue this ocean disposal was up for renewal. We had some misgivings about reapplying, but we went ahead anyway, in spite of public objections, because the technical data supported our position that the disposed materials did not harm marine life.

But in hindsight, we can see that we weren't sensitive enough to the views of the people living on the New Jersey coast. They didn't care about our technical data. They oppose ocean disposal of any sort because their coastal region represents a valuable economic resource as well as a recreational area.

Our Corporate Agenda

I like to think that a response of that nature represents the basic ethic of our company. We cannot sit around and wait for events to drive us. We, along with other manufacturers, must develop a corporate agenda for environmental leadership for the next decade.

Our agenda at Du Pont calls for us, by the end of the century or before, to reduce total hazardous waste in manufacturing by 35 percent, manage at least 1,000 square miles of land to enhance the habitat for wildlife, eliminate heavy metal pigments used in the manufacture of some plastics, take increasing responsibility for the environmentally acceptable disposal of the plastic portion of the global solid waste stream, to involve community representatives in discussions of present and planned local plant operations relevant to public health or the environment, and to consider environmental performance—both pro and con—in determining compensation of company managers. Our objective is to make Du Pont one of the world's most environmentally sound manufacturing companies.

Industry needs to maintain the same high environmental performance standards regardless of the country of operation. The actions of any one company will continue to reflect on industry as a whole. It's fair to say that manufacturers around the world are in this together.

Industry has a checkered past in environmental matters, and as a result, manufacturers have been painted many colors in recent years. That will have to change. In the future we will have to be seen as all one color. And that color had better be green.

Edgar S. Woolard is chairman of E.I. duPont de Nemours and Company.

Chapter 39

Ryder's Success Formula: People + Principles = Performance

by Ron Dunbar

*E*xcellence in Ryder is not a vague, idealistic goal. At Ryder excellence is a reality—it is a standard of performance that we are expected to achieve. We have a commitment to high performance that is understood and, more importantly, shared by our people. Ryder people expect to excel.

It is this commitment to excellence, this determination to do the best job possible, that makes Ryder a leader in its industry—a company that is as ethical as it is profitable.

Management Principles

Our goal, "Growth through Excellence," means many things in a corporation—growth in products and services offered, growth in financial strength, growth in earnings and revenue—but "Growth through Excellence" also means personal growth. When people join Ryder, they know that if they meet the high standards of Ryder excellence, they will be rewarded and given opportunities to further develop their skills and their career potential. This is an implicit understanding we have with our employees.

The focus for Ryder's commitment to excellence in both business and individual performance is the Ryder Management Principles. These principles represent the values, ethics, and expectations that permeate all activities of the company.

First, they form the foundation of our business and human resources philosophy. Second, they direct us in the management of our business and our employees on both a long-term and a day-today basis. Third, they define what the company expects from us and, in turn, what we may expect from the company.

Business Performance

The overall excellence of our people is best measured by the total business performance of our company. Consider the hallmarks of an excellent company: financial strength, profitability, strategic planning, new product development, customer service, market leadership, and employee productivity.

To excel in each of these areas, a company must have intelligent, dedicated, and productive people. It is the cumulative and continued actions of such people that create and sustain success.

Internal strength is unquestionably vital to success. Equally vital is external perception—the manner in which we are viewed by potential investors and customers. The strong long-term performance of Ryder stock and our ability to acquire capital are dependent upon how well the financial community, as well as our customers, view the quality of our management and the productivity of our people.

Adherence to the Ryder Management Principles will not only further reinforce our internal strengths, it will also enhance our external image as a high quality, ethical company, and will result in continuing growth and profitability.

A review of the Principles that guide our business actions and decisions demonstrates this clearly:

• To provide the very best product and services possible within the bounds of economic acceptability.

• To be a positive contributor to our customers in the accomplishment of their objectives.

• To make a fair profit for our stockholders on a continual basis.

• To obtain the best value from our suppliers in an honest and forthright manner.

• To conduct our business within established legal and ethical bounds.

• To establish and maintain high standards for ourselves and our organization units.

• To be a positive contributor to society.

The Management Principles both require and reward certain standards of behavior and performance for Ryder managers and employees. While the primary responsibility for ensuring that the Principles are followed rests with the individual manager, our people share ownership and responsibility.

Ryder has earned a national reputation as an excellent company for success-oriented individuals. The quality, pace, and standards of our company attract people who have the talent, drive, and ability to succeed in the Ryder culture.

In addition, our managers recognize that the recruitment and selection of the best possible people is critical to the ongoing strength and growth of the company.

This practice of hiring and promoting only the best performers not only ensures our management strength in the future, it enhances our ability to attract and retain the best people in the work force today.

Ryder's future excellence is dependent upon its ability to develop the full potential of its human resources and have readily available a pool of capable and committed employees. This requires a two-pronged approach. First, on a short-term basis, is the training and education of employees who have the desire and potential to advance their skills. Second, on a long-term basis, is the effective implementation and use of Ryder's Succession Planning Program.

Succession Planning ensures that Ryder has qualified people available to fill key management positions. Succession Planning helps us identify "backup" talent and develop high potential employees; and it creates a data base of people who are ready to assume greater responsibilities. This program is currently being improved to include more accessible and accurate information about our management candidates, their background and skills, and their potential for advancement.

Training and education are handled through a variety of both formal and informal methods in RSI and the divisions. We offer a number of skill-specific, employee training programs. These include supervisory skills, effective communication, computer courses, sales training, driver training, mechanic certification, as well as apprenticeship and college intern programs. In addition, we offer a substantial Tuition Aid Program, cover expenses for outside seminars and workshops, and provide a great deal of on-the-job training and skill development.

Ryder also has a commitment to management training. Our Ryder Senior Management Program utilizes the latest research regarding the qualities and skills that characterize effective leadership. Also, a cross-divisional training advisory committee has been established to share programs and information, determine needs, and design new and more innovative training programs and techniques.

Pay for Performance is the keystone of Ryder's compensation structure. Pay for Performance enables our managers to reward excellence in performance through higher pay increases and increased promotional opportunities. The direct relationship between performance appraisal ratings and both merit increase and promotional percentages sends signals to our better performers: that their additional productivity is recognized and rewarded.

Ryder's management incentive plans represent another reinforcement of our Pay for Performance philosophy. These plans are leveraged to provide our managers with average income when business performance is average, and substantial income when business and individual performance are exceptional. There is a strong and direct relationship between company profits and the incentive rewards that are paid to the people who are responsible for those profits.

Rewarding performance and encouraging employees to share in the success of the company are evidenced in other income programs, such as:

• Commission plans, sales incentive plans, and productivity incentive plans

• Certification pay for mechanics and safety awards for drivers

• Stock option plans, restricted stock awards, and profit incentive plans for key executives.

• The Employee Stock Purchase Plan and the Employee Stock Ownership Plan, designed for wide employee participation.

Setting clear, challenging individual performance goals is critical to the achievement of excellent performance. At Ryder we measure individual performance against stated objectives and encourage the use of individualized performance measures for each job throughout the organization.

Ron Dunbar is the Senior Vice President of Human Resources & Administration for Ryder Systems, Inc.

Chapter 40

Can Nice Guys Finish First?

By Gerald A. Johnston

You've heard the phrase *Nice guys finish last* so many times that you're probably beginning to believe it.

How true is that? Well, it depends on what we mean by *nice*.

If we're unassertive and over-accommodating—soft, in other words—then we must expect to be left in the dust by aggressive competitors. But if we're principled, dependable, and respectful—a more disciplined *nice*—there's no reason why we can't come out on top. There are enough prominent leaders in this world to prove that theory.

The pity is that in certain quarters, considerate behavior was viewed as a quaint custom incompatible with the gladiatorial nature of a global business war. To be nice is to be ethical, and to be ethical is to put oneself at a disadvantage. What some people seem to be saying now is that "honest guys finish last."

That may lead us to wonder about our own beliefs. Is moral reasoning a detriment to winning at business? Does a code of ethics represent, as one cynic suggested, the way we'd like to act if only it were profitable? Is ethical behavior something we advocate simply because it makes us feel righteous?

We at McDonnell Douglas put those questions behind us many years ago by deciding without much hesitation that ethics should be a part of our fundamental values and not because we were interested in achieving sainthood. It's a matter of doing what's right, and of survival. And our position has not changed. We believe that strong ethics beyond just compliance makes good strategic business sense. Questionable ethical behavior inevitably leads to questionable business performance.

For that reason, there can be no compromise. Honesty and integrity are not simply the *best* policy. They are and must be the *only* policy.

Ethics has underpinned our endeavors from the moment that our founder, James S. McDonnell, opened the doors of the McDonnell Aircraft Company in St. Louis in 1939 with an enunciated vision to "make men," not exploit them. His sentiment set the course for our efforts with regard to the fair treatment of all employees. I'll tell you that Mr. Mac, as we called him, became a legend not only because of his extraordinary charisma but because of his towering integrity.

Decency and truthfulness were also the stock-in-trade of our other founder, Donald Douglas. He was a man who stuck to his principles adamantly. Dozens of anecdotes illustrate the value of a strong ethical code for our business. Take the high road, those stories tell us, and you won't go wrong. But sustaining high ethical principles takes hard work. It's no small job to make sure that we obey the law in everything that we do, follow the standards for ethical conduct we have set for ourselves, and offer support and encouragement to the ombudsmen who act as a sounding board for ethical problems throughout our corporation.

As COO, I have a particular responsibility for helping to set the tone for sound ethical conduct. One way, of course, is by example. Employees on the production floor will believe what their management says only as long as they see the words come to life in the behavior of their leaders.

Another is to ensure that teammates who know of ethical violations can report them without fear of reprisal. And we owe it to all parties to guarantee a fair and impartial hearing of disputes. Beyond that we seek to weave ethics into the fabric of our work culture, quietly and surely so that every facet of every operation is carried out with a keen sense of ethical awareness.

Sandy McDonnell, our chairman emeritus, who has spent much of his career stressing the importance of ethics, is fond of saying that no relationship can long endure unless it is based on ethical behavior. You may get away with cutting ethical corners in the short run, he says, but in the long run it's bad strategy—your business simply will not survive.

Sad to say, economic crisis can sometimes bring out the worst as well as the best in us. We all know that our industry is in a tough competition for survival right now and that the adrenaline is running high among the leading players. Such conditions create avarice and conflict, and there are those who work hard at turning political issues into ethical issues. We at McDonnell Douglas have felt the impact of sustained public scrutiny and criticism with respect to certain of our programs and products. But we can say that we have followed both the book and our good conscience in all our actions every day, and we have not done anything that in any way compromises our integrity, even slightly.

We have sought time and again in controversies to explain our position, to furnish appropriate data, to offer perspective in brief, to establish an accurate record of what has transpired. Sometimes our message gets heard, and sometimes it doesn't. It's something of a tragedy when we fail to properly communicate our point of view, because, as Shakespeare suggested, misperception lives on while the good that we do is often interred with our bones. It hurts when our good name is called into question, particularly when we have spent years building an ethical culture that frowns upon the appearance of impropriety.

Much of the problem can be traced to the growing adversarial atmosphere between business and government which affects our relationships with our government customers. Each of us, in business and in government, must seek an end to this destructive hostility and misunderstanding and work toward a system that promotes cooperation and partnership. Nevertheless, the call to prove oneself as an individual and a corporation is a process that never stops.

On the Personal Side

Ethics has affected me in a very personal way. During the recession in the aerospace industry, we experienced one of the most difficult periods in our corporation's history. Our workforce was reduced by about 37 percent. Another four percent were transferred to new companies as a result of asset sales.

That means that about 55,000 teammates had to begin a new life. I knew many of them. I'd worked with them, shared with them the pain and pleasure of setback and success. People came to me directly, begging for their jobs. How do you tell a person who has served our company for 20-plus years that they are no longer needed? In each case, I tried to explain in the best way I could that each layoff represented a decision we in management had to make to maintain our competitiveness, our quality focus, and to meet our customers' needs.

It was as if, in one moment, we in management were confronted with all the most complex ethical questions any corporation would ever likely face. People were angry and confused. Some felt betrayed and deceived. Never before did we need to be so diligent about weighing the rights of our employees, our retirees, our suppliers, our customers, and, not least of all, our shareholders. Naturally, we felt an ethical obligation to help departing teammates cope with the trauma of such a huge readjustment.

We were strongly committed to the cause of ethical behavior during this time of increased pressure. We created a Business Practices

Committee of top executives to make sure that ethical practices were observed, and to protect those who reported an ethics violation.

We also provided other ethics education. We tried to make ethics training more practical and realistic—and a little more fun—by using Martin Marietta's "Gray Matters" board game (created by George Sammet) to teach teammates how to sort out ethical ambiguities. Having played the game with my children and grandchildren, I assure you that the game stimulates a lot of healthy dialogue on ethics.

Like others in the defense industry, we at McDonnell Douglas have worked hard to improve the way we do business, because we want to survive and prosper. We want to do things right, in every sense of the word, and not merely because the law requires it.

Ethics, like the improvement of our systems and processes, is an essential part of our quality movement. Integrity is as much a part of our heritage as world-class craftsmanship and engineering.

So yes, nice guys can finish first. If our industry is to continue to lead the world, we have to believe that principled and decent behavior will always triumph over expedience and duplicity.

No relationship in our personal lives or at work can last unless partners treat each other with loyalty, generosity, respect, honor and trust. Let's see to it that we continue to foster those attributes in our daily work lives and keep ethics where it should be: at the foundation of everything we do.

I don't think there was anyone who brought the subject of ethics into better focus than Dr. Albert Schweitzer, who said, "In a general sense, ethics is the name we give to our concern for good behavior. We feel an obligation to consider, not only our own personal well-being, but also that of others and of human society as a whole."

Gerald A. Johnston is the retired president and COO of McDonnell Douglas Corporation.

Chapter 41

The Practical Idealist

By David K. Hart

*F*or too long we have denied the rigorous disciplines of ethics. To be a principled individual has always required both knowledge and moral courage; to be a principled society has always required sustained moral effort. But in our headlong rush for prosperity, we have trivialized the ethical standards of our national founding.

Self-indulgence has led us to devitalize the rigors of ethics. We have likewise devitalized the values that sustain such ethics.

But why should we have problems being ethical? Conventional wisdom has it that we learn about those unalienable rights as children, at our mother's knee. Ethical problems should, therefore, be easily resolved by simply refreshing our memories about what we already know. But therein lies the problem—for the ethics of the playground are most inadequate for the problems of adult life.

To illustrate, assume a CEO refuses to hire accountants, arguing that since all employees had budgeted their allowances as children, the accounting problems of the organization can be solved by the application of the same homely principles. That CEO would be dismissed as hopelessly irresponsible. But is that much different from the CEO who tries to resolve organizational ethical problems by urging a return to the moral rules of childhood?

I do not argue that we should hire "ethicists." But it is an irreducible fact that one must know the principles before one can act ethically. In too many organizations, ethics consists of combining the law with the homilies of childhood to construct a moral checklist. Such codes of conduct are splendid public relations, evidence to a skeptical public of the firm's essential "niceness." But they are no substitute for rigorous study and discourse. As a result, in our time, slogans do the duty for discourse, and "photo-opportunities" substitute for moral action. We are getting what we have paid for.

The revitalization of our ethics must begin with the rejection of the popular but crippling notion that ethics can be learned in childhood only. Such notions are most unwarranted, for not only can ethics be learned throughout a person's lifetime, it actually requires the concentration of a lifetime, else one cannot achieve genuine happiness. The next step in revitalization is to clarify what we mean by "ethics." For the Founders, it was intimately related to happiness, correctly understood. Happiness in contemporary America seems to begin with the income from a million dollars in protected investments.

This means that happiness comes through virtue: ethics consists of those principles of virtuous conduct, derived from the moral truth, the practice of which constitutes happiness.

If we are to take organizational ethics seriously, we must begin with the fact that there are no easy paths to ethics: it requires unending study, moral discourse, and the courage to apply the principles in daily actions.

Four Founding Values

Discussions about ethical standards in American organizations must begin with one overriding fact: we are bound, by an original contract, to the founding values. That contract is acknowledged in our quest for the original intent in the legal system, in the oaths of office in government and the military, and in our reliance upon the founding values as the basis for our claims to fundamental rights as citizens. For some, this may be an open issue, but unless we draft a new Constitution, we are bound.

I wish to emphasize the point made by Robert Frost—that every American, must engage in a continuing dialogue with the Founders to discover the truth of the founding values. Taking the dialogue a step further, I present four premises, common to the Founders, that should be the basis for all organizational ethics.

First, the sanctity of each individual life. There is a transcendent moral truth that is the necessary foundation for happiness. It is quite risky to suggest a single moral *a priori* that guided the Founders, but I believe it can be argued that everything was based upon an extended meaning of the first word in the Jeffersonian triad of "life, liberty, and the pursuit of happiness." Everything begins with the absolute sanctity of each individual's life.

In Whitman's powerful words: *Underneath all, individuals. I swear nothing is good to me now that ignores all individuals. The American compact is altogether with individuals, The whole theory of the universe is directed unerringly to one single individual—namely to You.*

Regardless how the Founders derived the entailments—through reason or moral intuition—the founding values rest upon that premise. It then illuminates both equality and liberty, and gives personal meaning to happiness. As free agents, individuals can magnify or squander the possibilities of their lives, but those lives are sacred. Therefore, no organization, public or private, has any right to deny, or even trivialize, the possibilities of individual lives with organizational requirements.

The Founders were not wishy-washy about asserting this ethical priority, believing it to be applicable to all peoples, in all times and places. They understood and accepted cultural relativism—that times and climes would shape institutions. But they would not accept any relative or situational modification in the higher reaches of the moral truth. Without understanding that passionate commitment, we cannot understand their intentions.

Second, public and private virtue. A free nation requires both public and private virtue. John Adams was particularly emphatic that a true democracy required virtuous individuals in both the public and the private sectors.

Reason, history, and experience had taught the Founders that virtuous character could not be legislated: laws could not compel virtue; they could only compel obedience. Hence, they argued for a political system that held moral rules to a minimum, but granted full opportunities for moral voluntarism. Following the Ciceronian axiom of *doing the right thing for the right reasons,* they knew that individuals must have both ethical knowledge and a voluntary desire to act upon such knowledge, if those actions and intentions were to fuse together into virtuous character.

Moreover, as they made clear, moral character cannot be compartmentalized: one cannot be an ethical swine at work and a saint at home. A facade may be maintained, but the lives of such individuals have no more integrity. Furthermore, one cannot be an unthinking automation at work and a true democrat in off-hours. Thus, just as moral thought and discourse must infuse every aspect of an individual's life, so also must moral voluntarism be central to every aspect of our national life, in both public and private.

Any time morality must be enforced by law or rules, we have failed as citizens. The tragic need for civil rights legislation was an indictment of our collective and individual failure to grant even rudimentary rights to our black brothers and sisters. How much better it would have been had we done the right thing without the necessity of compulsion. Issues like racism or sexism, malfeasance in office, or lying under oath should never arise in America because the founding values require virtuous conduct in all aspects of our lives.

Third, all organizations in our nation should be governed by the founding values. The Founders believed that all institutions—social, economic, and political—should be constructed and managed according to principles derived from the founding values. That would mean making them congruent with human nature, which would insure that people would be productive and happy. If they are not so constructed, people become alienated and unhappy.

The Founders understood Adam Smith's argument that people become what they spend most of their lives doing. And if their lives never transcend the manufacture of pin heads, then there they stay. Because most of our lives are spent in economic endeavor, when economic values are not congruent with the values of the political system, democracy is impaired. In short, a people cannot fully realize true democracy if they spend the days of their lives in authoritarian economic institutions, any more than they can realize true free enterprise in a totalitarian government.

Fourth, all citizens must be constant students of the founding values. The Founders hoped that future generations would care as much about moral philosophy as they did, and that they would, accordingly, study, argue and, believe in those values with the passion they themselves felt. They assumed that intelligent people would do their moral homework before they engaged in any significant enterprises. We have failed them miserably in this area. We are far too "practical," too "realistic," to have anything to do with moral philosophy, and so the vision has atrophied—and we know not why.

The Practical Idealist

The Founders were nothing if not practical men of affairs, but they were also first-rate students of moral and political philosophy. They exalted "experience" as a teacher, but that experience was filtered through informed and humane intellects. They studied history, moral and political philosophy, arts and letters—and from these came to believe in the eternal verities of "life, liberty, and the pursuit of happiness." They knew that such knowledge imposed upon them the obligation to act upon those principles. But action uninformed by moral truth leads eventually to moral disaster. Their vision was the "practical idealist"—the individual who understood that the learning of the practical must be matched by the learning of the ideal. They became their own vision.

For this reason, ethics must be the most fundamental subject taught, a prelude to a lifetime of progressive moral study. The moral truth must inform every goal, structure, and process of our lives.

David K. Hart is Professor of Free Enterprise Studies at Brigham Young University.

Chapter 42

The Service Ethic

By J. Irwin Miller

*L*eadership that is concentrated on the ideas of one person is very limited. Genuine leadership involves getting all the wisdom that is available in a group, and helping that group come to a better decision than any one of its members would have achieved alone. The servant-leader gets the best out of people in several ways.

• *Grow from your roots.* I moved back to my hometown because my family and roots were there. Living in a small town means to have some roots down. You're less isolated than you are in the big city. You still get to be part of a whole community.

At Cummins, we grew slowly, gained market share, and built a reputation for excellence. It required a humane corporate ethos that elicited the best efforts from all employees and helped them to work together as a team.

• *Keep an open door.* In business, money and machinery help, but they are inanimate creations of human beings. The real achievement is the creative and collective achievement of individuals working together. Cummins is a tight-knit company where everybody knows what the other person is doing; nobody runs a truculent little principality.

Workers with complaints found that my door was always open to them. I joined the mechanics at softball games and diligently bowled in the shop league just to ask them questions and hear their answers. The relative harmony in our company is due to the trust cultivated between management and labor over the years. I wouldn't know how to run a big company without a strong union. The unions are management's mirror. They tell you things your own people won't admit. I want to pick the best out of their contracts and keep away from those things that put limitations on the freedom of individuals to act and move.

• *Nurture the human spirit.* Business executives must develop gifts of human empathy and ethical sensitivity. At Cummins, we pioneered the recruiting of liberal arts graduates. If you head a business, you ought to have a lively curiosity about all parts of society—where it is heading, what the role of business is, and where your company fits. Curiosity is more important than technical training. The liberal arts teach you how you got where you are, and what the real values are, and what are only appearances. Then when you come up against the problems of your time, you can distinguish between the real values and fashion.

Management must engage the whole person. My approach does not draw upon utilitarian logic or industrial psychology—"how can I get person A to do B?"—but stems from a humanistic empathy and understanding of the inner capacities of people. Your life is apt to be fragmented unless you have some force in your life that ties together everything you do.

• *Hire and build character.* Character matters. Don't waste time trying to burnish a corporate image. Worry first about developing the inner values, sensitivities, and strengths from which will flow the necessary virtues for running a vigorous, responsive company. Corporate leaders must have an enormous stake in all character-building agencies and services in the community.

You don't know where a young Abraham Lincoln might be today. He could be down on the farm. And simply because he never was elected president or appeared in the press doesn't mean he's any the less an Abraham Lincoln either. There are many great men and women of whom no one ever hears, but who live great lives.

When selecting young executives, I want them to regard their jobs as life missions to serve the company, not as short-term stints to advance their careers. A company's long-term needs are often out of sync with the short-term nature of today's shareholder base. Cummins, or any company, must balance the interests of all stakeholders (customers, employees, suppliers, the community, and stockholders) because long-term prosperity depends upon the contributions of all of them.

• *Look within yourself.* I did not set out to create a model of anything. When a problem arose, we felt the need to help find a solution, and in the process, we set off a whole chain of events. That's about what happened. Assume an attitude of humility and look within yourself. Men and women must know, as never before, what they are about. They must comprehend with mind and heart and spirit who they are, how they got here, and what is the nature and the true worth of every portion of the inheritance which has been placed in their hands. The scientist, engineer, lawyer, teacher, or governor, loose in this world without the restraints of such wisdom and such understanding, is a pure menace in our midst, and a danger greater than that of the bomb or the missile—for bombs and missiles do not yet launch themselves.

• *Seek first wisdom.* Out of lack of wisdom, out of lack of understanding and broad knowledge, men are forever forgetting their true needs, ignoring their real interests, and rushing to embrace either acute or attenuated self-destruction. Look beyond immediate selfish interest to pursue a more visionary and voluntary self-interest. We executives, who are in such great need of wisdom, so often do not hear any voice save our own. Our own ideas and our own biases become enclosed in sanctuaries. Few challenge them. We permit no one to invade.

Either our industries will fulfill their moral obligation to minimize the threat of air, water, waste and noise pollution in this decade, or the people, led by our youth, will force the government to enact legislation requiring us to do the job we will not do ourselves.

• *Build the best.* Whatever you do, you better bring to bear the best minds you can find. Don't perform any act casually, build any building casually, or produce any product casually. Architecture has never been a token of prestige or image for me. Rather I see architecture as an organic expression of human needs—functional, social, and spiritual. The power of architecture to change habits is considerable. My aim has been to lift the human spirit and foster a harmonious community. The question I ask is, "What is good space for people?" Euripides said: "Where the good things are, there is home."

Business is not just about making money. The goal of all business enterprises should be about crafting a hospitable home for the human spirit. The good things in this world have never been the things we can hold in our hand and call ours. The good things for all of us always have been the good feelings.

• *Be pariahs on principle.* There are two schools of thought: Aristotle said ethics can be defined as the currently accepted practices in any society; Judeo-Christian tradition says there are certain principles of human behavior that are born in you. The rules of behavior are as inexorable as the laws of mathematics or physics; you violate them at your own peril. The most critical and perplexing problems in any association of human beings are truly moral problems. Our goal is to be fair and honest and do what is right, even when it is not to our immediate benefit. We are always prepared to be pariahs on matters of principle.

• *Adhere to business ethics.* Ethics is not a set of bromides or simple principles; ethics is the accretion of complex experience. You may start life with a collection of values and, like any person, you will violate them every now and again. But you really only learn about your values from your mistakes, when you try to make end-runs around them. You develop your convictions slowly. Your values become real only when they are tested.

Ethics cannot be a mere sub-discipline of public relations—a benign, conveniently vague creed that is too easily embraced by all. It must be a matter of total personal engagement and conscientious example. The personal example which we each offer in our daily lives, our daily actions, our daily decisions will outweigh in influence all the workshops, seminars, study groups, and speeches about the shortcomings of other people. And the burden of moral example falls disproportionately on those at the top.

The fundamental reason for business ethics is to do good long-term planning—to say, "What will I wish I had done if I could be around 50 years from now?"

In our home hang four portraits of family ancestors. These portraits remind me of each of the men who laid the foundation that I inherited. And if I don't do anything to build on their work, it hasn't been worth my time to take up space in the universe. The only really valid definition of *patriotism* I've ever found came from Tacitus, who called it "this praiseworthy competition with one's ancestors."

The artist is one of the most important and powerful influences in ethical instruction and always has been. There's an ethical content to the work of every great artist. Business has been my medium for expressing sublime feelings and insights.

J. Irwin Miller, chairman of the executive committee of Cummins Engine Company in Columbus, Indiana, and was the recipient of the Business Enterprise Trust Lifetime Achievement Award.

Section V

How Can We Resolve Ethical Dilemmas?

Chapter 43

Honesty and Integrity Mixed with Wisdom

By Robert F. Bohn

With all your getting, get wisdom and understanding—you will then find greater happiness and success with people.

As an executive trying to model excellence, how would you respond to these statements?

1. Corporate CEOs must always be honest.

2. Honesty is always the best policy.

3. Living a totally honest life is living a life of integrity.

4. Rationalization is part of living a life of integrity.

5. Using wisdom is living a higher law than total honesty.

Tough Decisions

Our answers to these questions reflect our core values, and these, in turn, affect the quality of our decisions. I see a relationship between honesty, integrity, rationalization, and wisdom in the decision-making process.

Answers to the Questions

• *Question 1:* FALSE. For this statement to be true, I would have to believe that we should be honest 100 percent of the time. Remember the old advertisement about "Ivory Soap being 99.44 percent pure"? While the soap made us clean, it still wasn't 100 percent pure. I believe that we should be 99.44 percent honest, but I don't think it is possible or desirable to be 100 percent honest. A subsequent example will demonstrate a legitimate exception.

• *Question 2:* TRUE. A policy is designed to influence and determine decisions consistent with the core values, principles, and mission of the organization. I believe that honesty should be a guiding policy in the governance of our personal lives as well as any organization. But, there can be legitimate exceptions to the general policy. Knowing how to decide when to make the exception to any policy is the key.

• *Question 3:* FALSE. Living a honest life means that there is absolutely no deception. Whereas, living a total life of integrity means that we behave consistently with our core principles, values, and personal mission statement. Honesty may be at odds with our integrity.

• *Question 4:* TRUE. Sometimes we think only of the negative side of "rationalization" which has to do with devising self-satisfying but incorrect reasons for our behavior. However, we should not forget the positive side of rationalization which uses our brain in a reasonable and correct way consistent with our values and principles as reflected in our personal mission statement. In other words, using our rational brain-power wisely can enable us to live a life of integrity. Nevertheless, it is also very easy to slip into the "negative" side of rationalization and compromise our honesty inappropriately.

• *Question 5:* TRUE. Using wisdom enables us to know the appropriate exception to the policy of honesty. That is why Solomon counsels us: "Wisdom is the principal thing; therefore get wisdom: and with all thy getting, get understanding."

The Case for Nazi Germany

For example, suppose you were the CEO of an American corporation in Germany during the early 1940s. You found out that the Nazis were exterminating Jews; so, you arranged to hide some of your Jewish employees in the basement of company buildings. The SS officers barge into your executive offices and demand to know where all of the Jewish employees are.

How will you respond? If you are 100 percent honest, you will tell them where you hid the Jews. But, if you are 100 percent honest, you may not be living a life of integrity.

Wisdom is demonstrated by understanding how to choose between conflicting "good" principles. We do not have difficulty with such corporate decisions as: "Should we cut off the fingers of our employees?" Or, "Should we give them a raise?"

Choosing between "bad" (e.g., inflicting irreparable human damage) and "good" (e.g., rewarding people for performance) principles is easy most of the time. But, the challenge (including the requisite courage) for any executive is making wise decisions when two "good" principles are in conflict.

In the Nazi Germany illustration, the CEO had to choose between two conflicting "good" principles: "Being honest" vs. "respect for human life." If the CEO's personal mission statement incorporates correct principles and values, he will be more effective in making "wise" decisions. Living consistently with your personal mission statement is what integrity is all about. Wisdom is prioritizing our values and principles; then, we must have the courage to live with the consequences. In this case, choosing to lie to the SS officers enables the CEO to live a life of integrity because his priority for saving and "respecting human life" of his Jewish employees has priority over "being honest" to the Nazi officers.

We have the freedom to make decisions, but we do not have the freedom to choose the consequences of our decisions. Wisdom gives us the vision of the consequences of our decisions so that we have the commitment (and hopefully courage) to make the tough choices. By educating our consciences and getting understanding, we are able to better decide what is the greater good when two "good" conflicting principles collide.

This example uses hyperbole by focusing upon an extreme situation in Nazi Germany where wisdom would override honesty for the sake of integrity. Nevertheless, we must not lose sight of the over-arching principle of "honesty being the best policy" in 99.44 percent of the cases.

Using wisdom is living a higher law than total honesty because exercising wisdom helps us to be honest but not hurtfully honest. In other words, many people not willing to exercise wisdom can do great damage to those around them in the name of "total honesty."

Case of the Woman Executive

As the president of the corporation, you have finally promoted an outstanding woman to the executive team anticipating that someday she may become the CEO. She is new in her role as senior vice president and is very nervous about her first speech to the board of directors, wherein she will outline her plan for reorganizing the corporation. You have given her your total support.

Just before she walks into the boardroom, she asks: "How do you like my new outfit?" As a matter of fact, you don't like it very well. Should you be totally honest and say to her, "Frankly, I think it stinks"?

To make a "wise" decision, you need to think through the two conflicting good principles and the accompanying consequences. Accordingly, should you: 1) "be totally honest" and tell her that you don't like her outfit? or 2) "help her grow" by being less than totally honest?

Since honesty and growth are both part of your values and principles, how do you make a wise decision about the appropriate response you will give to your executive colleague? Learning how and when to choose between two good but conflicting principles is part of being an effective executive and leader.

Wisdom (prioritizing your values and choosing the greater good) suggests that you would tactfully say to her: "I can tell that you feel great in that outfit, and I know you'll give a fantastic speech." Although what you said was honest, it was not "totally honest" from the perspective of the "explicit" question she asked you. You withheld part of your perception because it could have devastated her confidence at that moment.

A wise decision is based upon personal integrity (behaving consistently with your prioritized values). In this case, you wisely chose her "personal growth" as the principle providing the greatest good in that moment.

Another aspect of this dialogue between you and your senior vice president is learning to sense what the other person is really asking. What was her "implicit" or real question? She was not really asking for your opinion about her dress. She was soliciting your support and approval as she was making an important speech. Being empathic (putting yourself in her shoes) is essential in knowing what another person is really asking.

In this case, your wise response is more honest (truly responding to what she is asking) than would be the seemingly "totally honest" reply to her explicit question.

The Virtue of Tact

Being sensitive to the needs of other colleagues enables us to use tact—the ability to appreciate the delicacy of a situation and to say the most fitting thing. Hopefully, important values in our personal mission statement will include respect and love for others.

To find the greatest good when faced with conflicting "good" principles, think through as many related values and principles as possible. Many people with little feeling for the other person's need will say and do things in "total honesty" which may be very detrimental to the other person. In fact, sometimes insensitive people can use "total honesty" as a brutal weapon to hurt other people—all in the name of being an "honest person."

Too often in life our most "natural" response (without wisdom) is not the most appropriate or helpful response. Tact requires judgment based upon our best wisdom. By using empathy, we can know what other people really need; and by living our life consistent with our core values and principles reflected in our personal mission statement, we can not only live a life of integrity, but we will bless those around us. Over time, wisdom will grow as we learn to choose the greater good in our relationships with other executives and subordinates.

Robert F. Bohn is chair of the Department of Financial Services and a professor at Golden Gate University in San Francisco, California. He is the past president of the Academy of Financial Services.

Chapter 44

Ethical Foundations

By William C. Ferguson

Not long ago the concept of "business ethics" was a novelty to most people. It was largely taken for granted by business executives, and it attracted little public attention except for an occasional critic. You may recall that George Carlin, the comedian, used to refer to "business ethics" as an oxymoron.

Times have changed. Ethics is center stage. The new federal sentencing guidelines have also helped raise the bar on risks for not taking proactive measures to apply and emphasize ethics. Ethics is among the most popular courses at Harvard Business School. It's top-of-mind with boards of directors, consumers, public officials, and the media.

It's also been top-of-mind at NYNEX, especially in recent years. We have always thought of ourselves as a highly ethical business going back to when we were part of the Bell System. Few people had any doubts about the Bell System's solid ethical foundation.

As much as I try not to live by the adage, "Adversity builds character," I find that, occasionally, it's true. In any event, we're a stronger business today because we faced up to a difficult situation and did a number of things to improve it. Hopefully, what we've learned will help you in your approach to ethics.

In 1988, a handful of executives associated with a materials purchasing company owned by NYNEX were operating "wild parties" in Florida, attended by some vendors. When we found out about these so-called "Florida parties," we took appropriate action. The executives involved were either fired or disciplined. We also notified our external stakeholders of the results of our own investigation and the steps we were taking to try to prevent this sort of thing from ever happening again.

Reflecting on this agonizing situation, I would pose this question: How much misconduct are you willing to read about on the front page of the *New York Times?* I have no more difficulty answering that question today than I did at the time of this controversy. As individuals and as business people, ethical behavior is a valuable asset, and at NYNEX, it's an indispensable part of our foundation.

As press coverage of the Florida situation continued to mount, it was clear to me that the people of NYNEX were facing what I would call a "crisis of confidence and trust" in one another. What appeared initially to be an isolated incident began to take on a life of its own.

As employees read headlines, they began to ask the question, "How could such a thing happen in our company? And, if it happened there, where else is it happening?" The ethics we had once taken for granted were being called into question, not only by the press but by our own employees. Even senior managers sitting across a conference table started to wonder if it was happening in the other person's shop.

I realized that we needed to look at the ethics issue in the broadest possible context. We needed to re-examine how we conduct every aspect of our business. Here are some of the things we did:

1. We established an Office of Ethics and Business Conduct at headquarters with a vice president in charge who has direct access to the chairman, with chartered responsibility to the Audit Committee of the Board of Directors. And there is a parallel office of Business Conduct in each of NYNEX's major business units.

2. Armed with the intelligence from our assessment, we drafted a unified set of standards—the NYNEX Code of Business Conduct to replace the separate codes that were in force throughout the family of companies.

3. We tested these new standards with nearly 2,000 employees to ensure that they not only covered the necessary issues, but were also clearly understood.

4. We then began conducting ethics training workshops, beginning with senior officers of the corporation including me. Our premise was that the ethics process has to start at the top and "cascade" down.

Gray Areas

I found out that ethics is something that many busy executives either take for granted or are reluctant to face. Most managers saw "bottom-line" or "hard" business issues as priorities—and ethics didn't make that short list. Other people felt that ethics training was unnecessary for them, and some saw it as a personal affront.

However, once the training got going, as dialogue developed on real-life issues we confront in our business, the participants began to discover there were many "gray areas." They began to realize that there were areas that needed clarification.

In gray areas, employees must make difficult choices, and they need help. Our response has been clear standards amplified by questions and answers, and supported by readily available guidance and clarification. Our goal is to try to keep gray areas from becoming problem areas. This is probably the most difficult task of all: Making ethics a living, breathing part of the way we conduct our business, an everyday norm.

We view continuous improvement in ethics as essential to the way we treat our customers, colleagues, and other stakeholders, including share owners regulators and public officials.

To take ethics for granted in this complex environment would be like taking quality for granted. And that is unthinkable.

Ethics is one of the critical values and priorities that define how we conduct our business along with quality, caring for the individual, cost-competitiveness and earnings growth. Just as we've been training employees on the importance of ethics and quality, we are now training people in what we call the NYNEX Winning Ways—the key behaviors and attitudes that help us exceed customer expectations and win in the marketplace. These behaviors start with integrity and leadership, emphasize communications and the power of diversity, and end with a strong sense of accountability. This is a lot easier to describe than it is to put into practice. There is a tendency to think of these behaviors as "soft" issues far removed from the "hard" bottom-line realities.

Once you start working on so-called "soft" issues like ethics, you find out that they're a lot harder than you thought. As management consulting gurus have been telling us, "soft is hard," because people tend to take the soft areas of business for granted.

Having worked on both "soft" and "hard" issues, I can tell you that there's nothing "soft" or "easy" about changing the way you do business any more than it is easy to get results in areas like earnings, costs, or service quality.

Moreover, unless you can change the "soft" things about your business, you're not going to be terribly successful in getting at the "hard" things you face. In fact, these two areas are intimately related to each other; the problem is that people don't think they are. So, "soft" is not only very important; it's often very "hard." But that doesn't discourage me. It only underscores how much ethics needs to be an ongoing and sustained effort.

We view guidance in the gray areas of our business as an essential target of the ethics process. That is where the right thing to do isn't obvious to many people, even after they have been exposed to an intensive ethics workshop, and have had their eyes opened up to what ethics really involves.

System failures are most likely to occur in the areas where the rules have not been clearly defined, have recently changed, or were poorly understood to begin with.

Four Lessons

Along the way, we have learned some things that may be helpful to you in your ethics process.

1. *There is a huge difference between "compliance" and "commitment."* That difference is especially apparent when it comes to ethics. If people are not seriously committed to ethics, expect to find them reading the ethics manual the same way W. C. Fields was reading the Bible: "looking for loopholes." If they're looking for loopholes, they're going to find them, no matter how good your code of conduct is.

2. *The best way to get that commitment is by getting buy-in on ethics through face-to-face communication.* Counter the doubters and skeptics (and that's most people) by forcing them to engage in a sustained dialogue about how ethics affects their conduct. You cannot force someone to take the ethics process seriously. But you can open their eyes if you have their undivided attention.

3. *Make sure ethics is part of an ongoing commitment—not just the "program of the month."* Make it clear to everyone that ethics is unconditional and a permanent part of the workplace—the one thing that needs to stay the same is the ethical way we conduct business. Ethics is the permanent platform for everything we are building.

4. *Leadership on ethics begins at the top.* The "shadow of the leader"—the role model that managers set for their employees—is the most important weapon in the ethics arsenal. My own "Law of Ethics" says that "The likelihood for unethical behavior in an institution varies in direct proportion to the degree of imperialism shown by management." Imperial behavior has no place in business. If managers expect others to be ethical, they need to practice what they preach. They need to cast an ethical shadow throughout the organization.

We make ethics the cornerstone of how we conduct business by practicing ethical behavior in our personal lives, in our business lives, and in our relationships. Ethics is a prime requisite for long-term success in whatever we are trying to accomplish. That applies as much to successful individuals as it does to successful businesses.

Our challenge is to live that ethical commitment every day—not just by saying it but by practicing it. As business people, we can't afford to do otherwise. In a world where change is a constant, ethics is the permanent foundation of our success.

William C. Ferguson is chairman and CEO of NYNEX Corporation.

Chapter 45

Ethics in Business

By Robert D. Haas

*I*n every facet of contemporary life, it seems that people are placing self interest ahead of ethical values. Pick up almost any edition of the *New York Times* and accounts of faltering ethical standards are chronicled.

Not long ago everyone had proclaimed that the "greed is good" spirit of the 1980s was dead and that the 1990s represented a return to basic values. But an honest evaluation of current business conduct contradicts that assessment.

Many incidents have led to an erosion of public confidence and an eruption of distrust in the major institutions of our society, including business.

While price fixing conspiracies, bribery, fraud, and business collusion are not the norm of contemporary business practice, they occur far more frequently than we care to acknowledge—and clearly more often than is permissible to gain the level of public trust and support that business requires to thrive.

What is most puzzling about instances of business wrongdoing is that they clearly contradict both the values that are held by most of us as individuals and the collective standards we have established for appropriate business behavior.

In his famous essay on civil disobedience, Henry David Thoreau wrote that a corporation "has no conscience, but a corporation of conscientious men is a corporation with a conscience." Still, how do we help honorable men and women confront and address the ethical challenges they face in the every day world of work? This is the puzzle all of us must work to solve.

Just as Adam Smith's *Invisible Hand* makes the marketplace a cruel taskmaster for the greedy, the inefficient, the manipulative, and the cheat, so the new realm of the informational economy will exact its toll on those who attempt to violate its systematic integrity or treat it with ignorance or venality.

This may be why so many young people are now taking to computers with such alacrity. They are discovering in them something that may have been missing in their lives—order, harmony, logic. Their parents may have given them uncertain guidance in right and wrong, but the ethical trumpet of the computer is never muffled or unclear.

All of which points to a fundamental fact: the only government possible in this new world-wide, free-wheeling, freely accessible information society is individual self-government, and such self-government will be imposed to a considerable degree by the technology itself. Increasingly, all other forms of government will remain viable only so far as they do not interfere with the unregulatable and illimitable systems of mind.

The only thing that interferes with this *Invisible Hand* of the self-disciplining marketplace is government's clumsy attempts to insulate us from it or to meddle in it. Black markets and their ancillary forms exist only because government tries to regulate prices or supplies. Bribery and extortion are the direct result of regulation, taxes, and licensure. Most white-collar crime depends on government regulation to support it and tax policies to make it profitable. It is excessive government by men, instead of by laws, that breeds lawlessness and venality.

Main Street values still live, but they do so in spite of the modern pseudo-moralists of both church and state who have left vast numbers of youth ill-equipped to deal with the evolving information society with its growing demands for self-discipline and integrity of thought and action.

Without the renewal of individual values, without standards and discipline, without the spiritual as well as moral education of the individual soul, the nations of the West will no longer be able to lead. They could self-destruct. Wisdom and science are implacably ethical and demanding. In an information age, the quality of our thinking will directly affect the wealth of our nation, even more than it always has. Jefferson warned: "If a nation expects to be ignorant and free, in a state of civilization, it expects what never was, and never will be." He understood better than most that even in the vast untapped material resources of the New World, true wealth was always more a function of what you know, than what you have.

Clearly, all of us feel strongly about ethics in the abstract. But each of us is keenly aware of the struggle we face as ethical dilemmas arise—the common struggle between our own desire to be ethical and the competing pressures of business performance.

We at Levi Strauss & Co. struggle every day with how to create a business culture that promotes ethical behavior.

Each of us can offer our own ideas about how to help managers and employees apply their own high ethical standards in the workplace, so that they don't have to check their values at the door when they show up for work.

Three very different approaches to dealing with ethical dilemmas characterize how companies approach ethics:

1. Neglect. It's hard to imagine that any large company could rationally ignore the importance of ethics or fail to develop management policies and programs given the effect ethical breaches can have on financial performance, sales, and corporate reputation. But some companies clearly don't get the message.

According to the Institute for Crisis Management, more than half of the news crisis stories are crises brought on by the questionable judgement of management—firings, white-collar crime, government investigations, and discrimination suits. Obviously, there are grave consequences for ignoring ethical problems. There is also increasing evidence that show positive correlations between responsible business behavior and return-on-investment, stock price, consumer preferences, and employee loyalty.

A company cannot sustain success unless it develops ways to anticipate and address ethical issues as they arise. Doing the right thing from day one helps avoid future setbacks and regrets. Addressing ethical dilemmas when they arise may save your business from serious financial or reputational harm.

2. Compliance-based programs. Compliance-based programs, most often designed by corporate counsel, are based on rules and regulations, with the goal of preventing, detecting, and punishing legal violations. Until recently, we were among the companies that took this approach. The centerpiece of our efforts was a comprehensive collection of regulations that spelled out our worldwide code of business ethics. In it, we laid out rules for hiring practices, travel and entertainment expenses, political contributions, compliance with local laws, improper payments, gifts and favors. We addressed topics ranging from accounting practices to potential conflicts of interest. As you might guess, it was a long and weighty list of do's and don'ts.

This approach didn't serve us well. First, rules beget rules. And regulations beget regulations. We became buried in paperwork, and any time we faced a unique ethical issue, another rule or regulation was born. Second, our compliance-based program sent a disturbing message to our people. Finally, it didn't keep managers or employees from exercising poor judgment and making questionable decisions.

We learned that you can't force ethical conduct into an organization. Ethics is a function of the collective attitudes of our people. And these attitudes are cultivated and supported by at least seven factors: 1) commitment to responsible business conduct; 2) management's leadership; 3) trust in employees; 4) programs and policies that provide people with clarity about the organization's ethical expectations;

5) open, honest, and timely communications; 6) tools to help employees resolve ethical problems; and 7) reward and recognition systems that reinforce the importance of ethics.

Ultimately, high ethical standards can be maintained only if they are modeled by management and woven into the fabric of the company. Knowing this, your challenge and mine is to cultivate the kind of environment where people do the right thing.

3. Principle-based approach. This method combines functional values with individual responsibility and accountability.

So, today, we base our approach to ethics upon six ethical principles—honesty, promisekeeping, fairness, respect for others, compassion, and integrity. We address ethical issues by first identifying which of these ethical principles applies to the particular business decision. Then, we determine which internal and external stakeholders' ethical concerns should influence our business decisions. Information on stakeholder issues is gathered and possible recommendations are discussed with "high influence" stakeholder groups, such as shareholders, employees, customers, members of local communities, public interest groups, and business partners.

This principle-based approach balances the ethical concerns of these various stakeholders with the values of our organization. It is a process that extends trust to an individual's knowledge of the situation. It examines the complexity of issues that must be considered in each decision, and it defines the role each person's judgment plays in carrying out his or her responsibilities in an ethical manner.

We're integrating ethics with our other corporate values—including diversity, open communications, empowerment, recognition, teamwork, and honesty—into every aspect of our business from our human resource practices to our relationships with our business partners.

The answers have become clear: Ethics must trump all other considerations. Ultimately, there are important commercial benefits to be gained from managing your business in a responsible and ethical way that best serves your enterprise's long-term interests. The opposite seems equally clear: the dangers of not doing so are profound.

Michael Josephson, a noted ethics expert, defined ethics this way: "Ethics is about character and courage, and how we meet the challenge when doing the right thing will cost more than we want to pay."

The good news is that courage carries with it a great reward—the prospect of sustained responsible commercial success. I thing that's what each of us wants our legacy to be. And I believe ultimately our key stakeholders—all of them—will accept nothing less.

Robert D. Haas is chairman of the board and chief executive officer of Levi Strauss & Company.

Chapter 46

Moral Dimension of Competitiveness

By C. J. Silas

Over 56 years ago, two American aircraft carriers, the *Yorktown* and the *Lexington,* were steaming toward a "rendezvous with destiny." Their mission was to defend the approaches to Australia from a Japanese invasion fleet. If they had failed, our strategic position in the South Pacific would have been in dire peril. When the four-day Battle of the Coral Sea was over on May 8, 1942, we had stopped the Japanese navy cold. Australia was safe.

Today, America is once again headed toward a rendezvous with destiny. Only now, the contest is economic. Ironically, many of the microchips upon which America's fast carriers rely, are "made in Japan." Various theories have been offered to explain how we got into this fix. And various proposals have been suggested for getting us out. And even if we were to adopt all of these solutions, we would still be overlooking the heart of the problem. I call it, "The moral dimension of competitiveness."

A Crisis of Character

What America lacks today is not just investment capital—it is character. We don't need a new industrial policy. We need more backbone. In his book *The Decline and Fall of the Roman Empire,* the great eighteenth century historian Edward Gibbon identified moral decline as the real culprit behind Rome's collapse. In America today, we don't have far to look to find evidence for Gibbon's thesis: our crime rate is appalling; sexually-transmitted diseases are helping drive health-care costs into the stratosphere; our children spend more time watching television than they do in school. From Wall Street to main street, and from the Congress to the county courthouse, many of our most prominent and respected citizens are getting caught cutting the ethical corners too closely.

Most executives are moral and ethical. Their faces, will never appear on the cover of *Time* or *Business Week* associated with some new scandal.

Instead, I want to speak briefly and narrowly to the kind of ethical dilemmas ethical people like you are likely to lose sleep over during your careers. The moral challenge imposed on you by a corporate culture can be subtle. The road to criminal behavior can easily be paved with good intentions. Consider these three actual cases:

• First, a plant manager at a glass-container plant in Gulfport, Mississippi, was found to have inflated the value of his plant's production by 33 percent. When asked to explain, he confessed that he was afraid the company would close this aging plant. That would have thrown him and 300 other employees out of work.

• In the second case, managers at a major auto plant were caught performing unauthorized maintenance on engines undergoing federal certification tests. They wanted to make sure the engines would pass government emission standards. When asked "Why?," these managers reported that senior management "put the squeeze on them" to get the engines certified.

• My third example comes from another automaker's truck plant in Flint, Michigan. Three managers had installed a hidden control box in a supervisor's office. The box allowed them to secretly speed up the assembly line. They did this to meet the production quota set for them by senior management.

It's a lot harder to resist temptation when honesty and integrity could mean the end of your town. And yet, those in top management need to realize that their decisions can foster sloppy morality. We tell managers to "improve productivity, but take no short cuts." Or we tell them to "cut costs but don't shortchange the customer." Objectives like these may be worthwhile, even necessary. But when you issue orders to subordinates, make sure that your people have the tools and resources to achieve these goals, ethically.

The Real Tragedy

The real tragedy of examples like these is not that people get caught and have their careers ruined. The real tragedy occurs when people are *not* caught. Because that means the company—or the school or the professional enterprise—has a false sense of how well it is actually doing. It's declining competitiveness or lack of quality remains invisible to senior management. Problems that could have been resolved easily early on get worse and worse, like termites in the woodwork. Then, when your company steams into its "Coral Sea," you will sink even before your competitors open fire.

These examples all involve clearly immoral or even illegal behavior. There is another category of moral decision in the business and professional world that is even more difficult to deal with. Business decisions have social consequences. Closing a plant can destroy a community. But operating an obsolete plant can cause environmental pollution. Failure to deal fairly with both sides of this issue can cost a company dearly. By ignoring the social dimensions of our decisions, we run the risk of losing the power to make our own decisions. If we are not careful, the regulators, politicians, and lawyers will take over.

Again, the most serious consequences for the nation will not be the immediate concerns at hand—the declining town or polluted river. The most serious consequence will be to our national competitiveness. When business acts on the premise that "if it's not illegal, it must be ethical," politicians will respond by piling on new laws and regulations. If we don't act ethically in those areas where the choices are up to us, we may lose the right to choose altogether. American business will find itself even more snarled in red tape and regulation than we are already.

Ethics goes beyond what you may have learned in Synagogue, temple, or Sunday School. It is about more than keeping the Ten Commandments in our private lives. What we are all called upon to do, whatever professional field we have chosen, is to make ethics the heart of every decision we make, from the boardroom to the mailroom.

C. J. Silas is chairman and chief executive officer of Phillips Petroleum Company.

Chapter 47

Power of Women to Stop Unethical Acts

By Karen E. Claus

*I*n April 1792, President George Washington took a stand that made a lasting difference in our government: he used his power to veto a bill passed by congress. Of course, his successors have been less reluctant than he to use their veto power to stop legislation they feel is inappropriate. For President Washington, and for all the chief executives since, the veto became an important source of power.

Women also have a veto power—the power to veto wrong-doing. They have a special sensitivity to evil and have the power to crush it. With this power also comes the responsibility to do so. If a woman will use this power—and teach others by precept and example to use it—then it will bless her life and benefit the lives of those around her.

For the most part, secret pacts, shady business practices, and other manner of wrongdoing have not set well with women. Women "show no compassion" for such activities.

In my opinion, if a woman does not use her "veto power," she may be aiding and abetting the wrong doing that she observes. When it comes to evil and unethical behavior, there is no neutral ground.

In the law, if people do not use the power that they have been given and for which they have a duty to act, it is called "guilty acquiescence" or "complicity." Acquiescence is implied consent. It is tacit acceptance or concurrence. Failure to make objections is acquiescent behavior. It is also legally considered complicity, that is, participation in guilt, and is one of those elements that must be proved in conspiracy or when someone is an accessory before the act of a crime.

If we are given a talent or gift, we are expected to use it. When we are given a gift of sensitivity to evil and unethical behavior, we have a right and duty to act, to use our gift to stop evil at the source.

I know a professional woman who has many skills and is physically beautiful. She did not protest when her husband began to see a younger woman in the hope of keeping peace in the family and stability in the home—thinking that the problem would go away. Unfortunately, the situation only got worse, and now there is a broken home.

Evil does not simply go away. When women and men sense an ethical problem at home or at work, they must do something about it. The immediate repercussion may be unpleasant, but the long-term gains will be positive.

Women have special gifts and qualities of character that make them better suited not only to child bearing and rearing but also to teaching and training in proper principles.

Ten Studies Verify the Point

Several studies of managerial behavior and ethics show that there are some basic behavioral differences between men and women on ethical issues. I have selected 10 studies to illustrate the point.

Study 1. Michael Betz, Len O'Connell, and Jon Shepard found that men were more concerned with money and power as career goals at age 40 than were women, who cited growth and stimulation as their career goals. The study found that more females wanted to help and to enter into relationships with others on the job. With regard to work-related values and interests, men were more concerned with money and advancement while women were more interested in relationships and helping others. Men were twice more likely than women to engage in the following five behaviors: using a shortcut in an estimating procedure that was opposed by the employer, padding travel expenses, selling marijuana, engaging in insider trading, and embezzling money via the computer.

Study 2. Jan Grant reviewed six qualities with regard to women's experience in the family, community and economic and political organizations.

• *Communication and cooperation.* Women tend to take turns in group discussion whereas men tend to seek to compete for the floor. The new emphasis on worker participation and "quality circles" in the work world will demand more cooperation, apparently a natural feminine tendency.

• *Affiliation and attachment.* Women tend to fuse identity with intimacy, whereas men seek independence and individual activity. Women concentrate on processes that allow people to work together more productively, whereas men concentrate on goals, tasks, and philosophy.

• *Power.* Women tend to see power as a transforming force within the person or as a liberating force in the community. Women view power as dependent on both sides of an interdependent relationship. They know intuitively that without a follower there can be no leader. Women tend to equate power with giving, caring, nurturing and serving, and tend to see these aspects as strengths. Men tend to look at power in a hierarchical manner. They equate power with aggression and assertion and think that the exercise of power requires the expenditure of much energy to control and limit others.

• *Physicality.* Familiarity with physical cycles and natural seasons make women more understanding and tolerant of organizational problems in day-to-day operations. Childbirth creates a new set of problems and a sense of companionship with women who have experienced the same life-changing event.

• *Emotionality, vulnerability, lack of self-confidence.* Men don't like to admit weaknesses because they feel this knowledge will be used against them. Women more freely admit their weaknesses and, therefore, are better able to work with them and to make improvements. Accurate assessment of strength and weakness is vital, as it can add a humanizing dimension and enhance the quality of life in organizations. The trend toward creative expression and humor in the workplace may be feminine contributions.

• *Intimacy and nurturance.* Women show greater capacity for empathy. They experience themselves as less separated from others and more connected to the world. Men, on the other hand, feel separated, tend to undervalue nurturance and skills in interpersonal relations and creativity.

Organizations that do not force women to fit the male managerial model may become more humane, less alienating and more responsive to all employees.

Study 3. Adamson and Associates studied physician communication skills and malpractice claims for insurance companies. They found that women and better educated patients preferred more explanations and were less likely to file malpractice claims if these explanation were given. Men and less educated patients preferred more authoritarian, dependent relationships with their physicians. These doctors also had more claims filed against them.

Study 4. James Harris found that women professed a utilitarian approach to ethics (the greatest good for the greatest number), focusing on a societal view when making ethical judgments. Men prefer an egoist or self-centered approach to evaluating outcomes of ethical judgments. Women dislike the cronyism or "old boy" system as they often fall victim to that system, whereas men prefer that type of fraternal association. Women think in terms of what is good for the majority; men try to maximize self-interest.

Study 5. In studying ethical judgments in marketing professionals, Akaah found that men reflected consistently higher approval for authority and position, even if the position taken by authority was unethical. Women showed higher ethical judgments than men. For example, women were most opposed to precoding supposedly anonymous questionnaires with ultraviolet ink, using ads that encourage consumers to misuse a product, or unwillingness to share data with community groups such as intercity advisory groups.

Study 6. John Barnet and Marvin Karson explored stages of careers and values with regard to executive decisions and found that women in the middle stage of their career were the most likely to be ethical. Men in their early stages were the least likely to be ethical. In all stages of career development, women were more ethical than men in terms of their values and decisions with the biggest differences being at the early stage.

Study 7. Marvin Karlins studied academic dishonesty. Of approximately 600 students studied, 22 students cheated (plagiarized) and were subject to disciplinary action by the university—21 of the 22 were men.

Study 8. Brenner found that women middle managers no longer sex role stereotyped the job of a manager and were more likely than men to treat men and women equally in selection, promotion and placement decisions. Male managers judged the job of a manager in terms of male characteristics and preferred males in the role of manager. This could explain the phenomenon of the "glass ceiling" that women executives experience on their way to the top.

Study 9. George Riley studied gender bias of the case method in business education and found that the case method requires more aggressive, competitive behavior and that men tend to dominate the discussion. Women tend to avoid conflict in case discussions and open competition. Women are also more likely to be called upon by their instructors. Generally the case method approach tended to favor men because of these factors.

Study 10. In her book *Political Women*, Jean Kirkpatrick surveyed politicians and found that women politicians, like the men, were very willing to fight for their convictions. Women, however, see power as an instrument of public purpose, whereas men tend to see power as a tool for personal ambition.

These studies show that men tend to be more aggressive; concentrate on goals, tasks and philosophies; see power as control and assertiveness; are unwilling to admit weaknesses; and tend to be more individualized in their approach. Women are more concerned with relationships; with the growth and development of others; with nurturing; and with fairness in the evaluation and promotion of others. Women tend to see power as working together, as a symbiotic relationship. Women are more willing to admit their weaknesses and more able to develop weaknesses into strengths.

What Is Power?

Power is composed of three interrelated elements: strength, energy, and action. When any of the three elements is missing, there isn't the critical mass needed for true power.

Ability and capacity derive from strength. Willingness derives from energy. Changes in performance derive from both action and movement. Strength yields ability; positive energy yields a willingness to act; and action itself yields results, the influence on other people.

Ability is based on strength. A powerful person has a self concept based on a realistic assessment of strengths and weaknesses. If men and women are humble, over time their weaknesses may become strengths. Where there is strength, there is also weakness.

Willingness is based on positive energy. A powerful person radiates energy, uses her own potential to the fullest, and sees both strengths and weaknesses in others.

When ability is backed by will, action will influence the performance of others. Power is based on results, on performance. Powerful people affect the behavior of others, and these effects can be observed and felt.

I view power as a pyramidal force: strength supports energy, which supports action. Strength, energy, and action are synonymous with the words, "can," "will," and "do." And I have found that "I can do it" and "I will do it" are prerequisites to "doing it."

Power is also a motivator. In men, the need for power is greater than the need for achievement. Most managers need power and like to use (and abuse) it. Such power must be a positive force encompassing individual strength, energy, and action. There must be a willingness to take actions and to influence others—a positive mental set toward using power effectively.

Women have a special role. To be a woman at this time is a challenge, but if met well, a woman's influence can be ten-fold what it might be in more tranquil times. Women have a special gift of sensitivity for what is good and profitable in this world—a special gift to raise children and to train people. This gift appears in women all over the world.

Women and men will be held accountable for their use of their talents and gifts. Deep within each woman is a special sensitivity to ethical principles, a keen sense of right and wrong. It is, therefore, our responsibility to stand and be counted in these very difficult times.

This standing for what is right starts in our families and in our interpersonal relationships with those who are around us wherever we are.

As stated in Proverbs, the price of a virtuous woman is far above rubies. As more and more women in the workplace stand for what is right, we will make a difference. By exercising our veto power over wrongdoing, we can change the world for the better.

Karen E. Claus is a visiting professor in the Institute of Public Management, Marriott School of Management, Brigham Young University.

Chapter 48

Ethical Fitness

By John W. De Pauw

William Haggett, CEO of Bath Iron Works (BIW) in Bath, Maine, effectively ended his career through a 15-minute ethical lapse.

My purpose in recounting Haggett's story is to focus on how good people make tough choices—or how good people at crucial times fail to do so, and pay the price.

In this instance, Haggett's 15-minute lapse cost him his career. BIW is one of the two domestic U.S. shipbuilders. The other is Ingalls Shipbuilding. The competition between the two companies for U.S. Navy shipbuilding contracts is fierce. One day, the fateful day for Bill Haggett, a group of BIW executives were together with Navy officials for a quarterly review meeting. A 67-page document, marked "Business Sensitive" was left behind by a consultant to the Navy attending the meeting. The document, containing page after page of their competitor's financial proposal, landed on Haggett's desk the next morning. Everyone knew that the document was legally forbidden information. But, after scanning the document for 15 minutes, Haggett discussed the contents with his executive subordinates.

Unfortunately for Haggett was that while he was gone, one of the subordinates had the good sense to tell the boss, BIW president Duane D. (Buzz) Fitzgerald, what was going on. Fitzgerald, a lawyer by training and sometimes called "the conscience of the shipyard," ordered the copy shredded and the computer data deleted.

Later, after conferring with Fitzgerald, Haggett delivered the original document to the local Navy officials. He did not volunteer to the Navy that he had copied the study. He only stated that "no copies existed." With this information, the Navy undertook its own investigation. Later in July its report concluded that no material damage had been done to Ingalls. Haggett and BIW were cleared of any serious wrongdoing.

Despite this "vindication," Haggett publically resigned his position as CEO. Ironically, Haggett did so, not at the insistence of the Navy, but at the urging of his own colleagues. Apparently they were so concerned about BIW's reputation for integrity that they asked Haggett to leave. Just 15 minutes of ethical uncertainty shot down his career. At the conference Haggett noted, "With the benefit of hindsight, I see it was a bad decision on my part."

A similar situation happened to Norman Augustine, chairman and CEO of Martin Marietta Corporation. While competing on a government contract, Martin Marietta mysteriously got a package in the mail with its competitor's bid in it. This was a day before the company was to submit the bid, so opportunities and profits seemed within easy reach. However, unlike Hagget and BIW, Augustine didn't "spend 10 minutes" debating what to do with the information. Not only did they turn the data over to the government, but the company also told its competitor what it had received. Martin Marietta lost the contract. Some employees lost their jobs, and the shareholders lost money. When asked if this was a case of a company being too ethical, Augustine was unequivocal in his answer. "No," he said. In the short run the company lost out. Nevertheless, Augustine recounts, "We helped establish a reputation that, in the long run, will draw us business." No career-ending move here, only a firm belief that a company cannot be too ethical.

What can we learn from these two stories? Perhaps the most important lesson is the need for, what Rushworth's Kidder calls, "Ethical Fitness." In the heat of an ethical moment, or moral challenge, the busy and harried executive must respond with a well-tuned conscience, a lively perception of the differences between right and wrong, an ability to choose the right and live by it. Such ethical fitness is not being mentally passive, but is being mentally engaged. It is being committed through emotions and convictions as well as through the intellect.

John De Pauw teaches for the University of Maryland. He is a managing partner in a consulting firm, and a partner in two other businesses.

Chapter 49

Your Role in Shaping Ethics

By Frank Navran

Can an individual make a difference? The question usually refers to the anonymous individual, the "little person" in the big organization. Most people assume that the CEO, president, vice president, or other senior executives can always make a difference. While the casual observer might think that rank brings power, it ain't necessarily so. Many people presumed to have power are powerless.

"I can't do anything—I'm just a vice president." These words were said by Mr. J., a vice president of a *Fortune* 500 company. He oversees 9,000 employees and has financial responsibilities for $30 million annually—and yet he complains that he can't change the organization to make it stop doing the wrong thing and start making it do the right thing because he does not have enough power.

He wants to create a more egalitarian working environment. He seeks to empower his employees, yet feels powerless to bring that change about. He believes that his hands are tied by union contracts, headquarters staffs, and tradition. He fears that any change would adversely affect financial performance in the short run, and be resisted by the other officers.

Once Mr. J. tried to change the ethical climate, but failed. He retired recently, relinquishing control of an organization not that different from the one he inherited 10 years ago.

The point of this story is to reframe the question: *Can an individual, regardless of title, power, or position make a difference?* I believe that every individual can make a small difference. Some individuals can make a large difference. The surprise is that the size of the difference is not a function of title, or position of presumed influence. It is a function of real power.

I define values as a system of beliefs—how one defines what is right, good, and fair. Ethics refers to how those values are acted out. Of course, "right, good, and fair" are hard to define. I am troubled by any person assuming the high moral ground and pronouncing "this is ethical" and "that is unethical." Yet I am equally troubled by the position that ethics is a function of situations. That position just feels too convenient. It is too easy to use situational ethics to rationalize that "what is best for me, now, in this circumstance, is ethical." Situational ethics is too easily abused.

Ethical behavior is acting in ways that are consistent with one's personal values and the commonly held values of the systems in which one functions (organizational, political, societal, religious). You might ask, "Was Hitler ethical because his actions were consistent with his values?" Or, "Are cannibals ethical because their society approves of eating other human beings?"

My answer is to refocus on the business world. I know many hard-nosed competitors, some who would celebrate the failure of another's efforts, but none who eat the remains of their competition. I know many petty dictators, supervisors who abuse their power and make their employees' lives miserable, but none who have those employees systematically murdered. The chauvinists and racists exist in business and are to be despised. By my definition, these aberrants are unethical, as was Hitler, because they violate various values of the society in which they are functioning.

Individual employees at all levels often feel expected or required to act in ways that violate their personal values. The result of these actions is harmful to the individual (the natural consequence of violating one's own standards for behavior) and harmful to the organization, its stakeholders, and society at large.

What Do Employees View as Unethical?

Employees judge ethics from a personal frame of reference. They judge an action to be unethical if it violates their perceptions of what is right, good, or fair. Organizational expectations and requirements to act unethically can therefore "legitimately" be ignored or thwarted. A good deal of creative energy is spent "beating" unfair systems and then protecting oneself from the consequences of doing what one believes is right, good, or fair contrary to stated or implied direction). This CYA (Cover Your Anatomy) behavior consumes vast amounts of resources.

Employees have to balance multiple sets of values. They bring their personal values to the job. They are subjected to their supervisors' values. They are taught the company's values, and they have to consider their (internal or external) customers' values. Unethical behaviors are those actions that violate whichever of these various values the employee embraces.

And it is always reasonable to expect that the employee's greatest allegiance will be to his or her personal values. Consider an employee who believes that the company's customer-service policy is unfair. This employee also believes that "Customer First" is right, good, and fair. She might choose to act in the customer's best interests, against the organization's instructions. She might bend a rule for a customer, or tell a customer how to escalate a complaint to get a fair settlement. The choice to serve the customer is judged ethical by the employee since she is doing the right thing in violating a policy or practice that she deems unfair.

But there is a price to be paid. Externally, the employee must face the wrath of a hostile organization. Internally, the employee pays a stress premium for breaking a rule, even an unfair rule.

How can people cope when they are expected or required to be unethical? The typical organization is losing $3,000 to $5,000 per employee per year to the retaliatory and self-protective (and often unethical) actions of employees who are caught in the dilemma of having to choose between conflicting definitions of right, fair, and good. Their coping mechanism is to sabotage what they judge to be unethical practices in order to maintain the integrity of their personal values—acts which they must rationalize as the lesser evil. Both they and the organizations pay dearly.

Yet the sabotage and self-protection remain covert. These individuals cannot make a difference, in the larger sense of influencing long-term change in the ethical systems of the organization, by remaining underground.

Ethics and Power

It takes power to create change or to make a difference. The bigger the difference you want to make, the more power it requires.

Organizational power comes from at least 10 sources: authority (position); obligation; coercion; personality; expertise; reputation; identification (association); resources; information; and rewards. Four of these—expertise, information, obligation, and reputation—are within the individual's control. So, the easiest way to become more powerful is to be more expert (be able to solve more problems), have and share more information (help others by knowing and sharing more), increase the obligations you are owed (be more helpful/do more favors for others), and reputation (earn trust and respect by demonstrating expertise, sharing information, being helpful, and keeping all promises).

Let's remember that organizational power is a perception. It is a self-fulfilling prophesy. If you think you have power, you are correct. If you think you do not have power, you are also correct.

Consider Mr. J. He had authority of position, but he lacked information and reputation. But his biggest failing was his belief that he could not bring this change about. "I can't do anything. I'm just a vice president."

Bridging the Ethics Gap

We call the difference between what people believe is right, fair, and good and what they believe is required for survival or success, the ethics gap. The ethics gap is responsible for sabotage and self-protective behaviors. Power alone cannot make a difference. It has to be intelligently and ethically used to enable the individual to make a difference. We have identified six steps that we think are required to bridge the ethics gap.

• *Be aware of the ethics gap.* Many employees ignore what is going on around them. They view their own acts of sabotage and associated self-protective behaviors, as well as those of the people around them, as business as usual. "That's just the way things are. It has always been that way. I can't do anything. I'm just a..." Nothing is going to change until someone acknowledges that business as usual is unethical and needs to be changed.

• *Define the gap.* Identify the values being compromised. Articulate which individual and values are in conflict with each other. Describe which routine decisions and behaviors, which expectations and requirements, are in conflict with the critical values of both the organization and its employees.

• *Develop ethically congruent alternatives.* Accept responsibility for thinking the problem through to conclusion. First consider alternatives that are congruent with your values and those held by the organization. Then do a rudimentary cost/benefit analysis on the more feasible alternatives. What are the benefits to the organization, its employees, and stakeholders? What are the costs? What would you recommend as a first step?

• *Develop a values-based argument in support of the most effective alternatives.* Consider what arguments would most likely appeal to the values of the decision makers? If they are bottom line oriented, what is the positive impact on the bottom line from ethical change? For example, would they be moved to support your alternative if it saved the company $5,000 per employee per year from reduced sabotage and self-preservation costs? If they are people-oriented, what benefits would the people realize from your proposal? If idealists, how does this change move the organization closer to living its ideals?

• *Join your power with others.* Take your ideas and conclusions to someone who has more or different power. Win the support of a champion. The logical first person is your immediate superior. Sometimes that person is part of the problem, and you cannot safely seek his or her assistance. If there is an ombudsman, or ethics committee, that is a great place to get more power. If not, use your associates, and their networks, until you have secured at least one powerful ally.

• *Escalate.* Move on to the next level. Continue to escalate the debate. Accrue more allies who bring more power and influence to the movement to make change happen. Rarely can individuals make a difference until they unite themselves with more individuals and eventually create the power of numbers.

What Are the Risks?

The "worst case" test asks three questions: What is the worst thing that could happen? How likely is it? How important is it?

A rational person would consider these three questions and make a rational decision. Zealots are not expected to be rational, and sometimes it takes a zealot to start the change cycle. The risks in becoming a change agent are real. In every organization, there are people with real power whose success is vested in the status quo. These people's power and influence come from using the existing systems (even the unethical systems) to advantage. They are apt to resist (or undermine) anything that they perceive as a threat to that power base (another example of organizational self-protection). They may even attack you, as the personification of that threat, seeking to discredit you (and thereby discredit the change you are proposing). That is why you need to align yourself with powerful champions.

Could you lose your job? Yes. Could you be demoted? Yes. Could you see your performance rating, income, or potential for upward mobility decreased? Yes. Are you willing to risk it? Only you will know how to answer that question when the time comes.

So, yes, the risks are real. But there are also protections. Being fired for threatening an unethical status quo is a wrongful act on the part of the organization. You might be entitled to legal protections. Many organizations have programs to encourage employees to raise ethical questions for executive review; they care about ethical congruence and helping employees to bridge the ethics gap. But others do not; and some even punish the person who makes a case for business-as-usual being wrong.

For some, being forced to leave a place that refuses to work towards ethical congruence with its employees is not an entirely bad thing. It might be an opportunity disguised as a punishment for wanting to live according to your values. These are individual decisions. The point here is to recognize that there are risks, some of which are well worth taking, and that you can reduce the risk level by the effective use of organizational power.

Yes, the individual can make a difference, but there are risks and the ultimate price can be high. But so can the price of not making a difference. Ultimately the reward of integrity, self-esteem and the worth of one's contribution to a greater cause might be higher than the short-term costs imposed by an organization seeking to maintain an unethical stasis.

Would I encourage you to take such a risk? I cannot say with the certainty that many of colleagues presume. I can only say that should you choose to make a difference, there are intelligent ways to use the power the system affords you to increase the likelihood of success and protect yourself from those who might perceive you as a threat.

To make that decision, first you must know what you care deeply about, deeply enough to make sacrifices, and then you must choose your path.

Frank Navran is president of Navran Associates, an ethics consultancy based in Atlanta, Georgia, and creator of Total Ethics Management *and* Bridging the Ethics Gap.

Chapter 50

A Return to Values

By Jeffrey R. Holland

*A*merican business and education have given the world two of its most distinctive and most encouraging ideas. American business proved on a broad, inclusive front that people could own land, exchange labor, accumulate wealth, and develop a system of commerce that would benefit not only a few privileged owners, but many, many of them—and the worker and the consumer as well—all regardless of class, creed, or color.

The American system of education also challenged prevailing attitudes about who should have access to the schools. Unlike any other place or period in the known world before it, education in America was to be education for all—regardless of sex or status or social privilege.

For nearly two centuries, the nations of the world have looked to us as the principal source of invention and creativity in these areas. Certainly they could see that the American experiment with democracy was giving more people increasingly greater access to material comforts, educational opportunities, and control of their own economic and political processes.

But in these past few decades, we have lost some of that international respect; indeed, we have lost some faith in ourselves. We seem to search everywhere for deliverance from a gloomy malaise that would make us believe that the nation which sent men to the moon and took snapshots of Saturn can't even agree on the cost of postage stamps or whether the mail will get across town at any price.

Business became the target of environmentalists and government regulation and suffered from foreign bribery scandals, accusations of social irresponsibility, and white-collar crime. Education was attacked for permissiveness, campus riots, grade inflation, irrelevant courses, and grim professionalism. Suddenly these two great forces that brought revolutionary ideas to the world had lost some of the trust and confidence of their nation. The movers and shakers had been moved and shaken.

Public opinion polls simply confirmed what many were feeling. In one survey released by *U.S. News and World Report* listing the institutions with the most influence on the nation as a whole, education ranked 23rd out of 30, just behind magazines and the movies. TV ranked 4th.

One Gallup Poll asked people which professions and occupations had the highest standards of honesty and ethics. Clergymen took first and car salesmen last, but businessmen were listed in the bottom ten!

I find it ironic that when most of the world is struggling to achieve the freedom from want already attained by the United States, we find ourselves troubled by a loss of faith in our economic institutions and leaders. Even more disturbing is the paralysis that seems to be associated with this pessimism. Nearly everyone talks about the "forces of history" or a feeling of decline that cannot be influenced or counteracted.

Shaping History

My purpose is to speak for influence and counteraction. I would want us to stand with those who shape history rather than simply yield to it.

If we want values at work or in school the same way we want values at home or in political life—and we haven't always had them there—we must realize that we cannot be passive in perpetuating these ideals.

Two simple reasons why people ignore standards is that they have never learned what the standards are or that they have learned that compliance with standards is not really an essential part of our expectation of them. We all know, or say we know, that honesty is the best policy. It's probably written in your company's code of ethics. But what most of us fail to do is to talk about it enough in our boardrooms, stockholder meetings, lunchrooms, or hallways in ways that make a substantial difference.

The same is true in education. I fear as a profession we've been unconscionably negligent in stressing morality, integrity, honesty, and ethics. In a survey of 131 U.S. business students, nearly all expected to face pressure toward unethical behavior, and fully one-half of them anticipated not resistance, but accommodation and compromise. We simply must do better. We must rediscover what Plato said in his Laws 2,400 years ago. "Education in virtue," he wrote, "is the only education which deserves the name."

Obviously universities used to have influence in the formation of proven values—that's why the *U.S. News and World Report* survey was so devastating to me personally: 23rd place out of 30, right behind magazines and the movies in influence.

A Concern for Ethics

If virtuous education is the only education which deserves the name, then perhaps virtuous business is the only business which deserves that name. Without concern for ethics—honesty, fidelity, and integrity required by the market mechanism—the free enterprise system itself breaks down, and society is then served by business poorly, or not at all.

In fact, Peter Drucker says that there is no such thing as business ethics—a code distinct and unattached from all other ethics. "There have always been a number of people who cheat, steal, lie, or take bribes," says Drucker. "But there [is] not [a] separate [code of] ethics for business, nor is one needed."

Drucker is simply confirming what a current popular magazine published—that it is foolish to worry about U.S. citizens cheating on taxes so long as an even greater number of Americans are cheating on their spouses. One code for the boardroom and another for the bedroom simply doesn't work.

The dangers of ethics just for business or education or politics are obvious. It becomes too easy to rationalize that, if the law or the teacher or the government or the board doesn't compel us otherwise, the sky is the limit. We then push larger, more permanent ethical considerations aside and recklessly go after the bottom line—whether that be a profit, a college degree, or a political office.

And, like the executive whose firm was accused of selling an unsafe toy, we justify our behavior on a new set of principles: "We broke no law," he said. "We're in a highly competitive industry. If we're going to stay in business, we have to look for profit wherever the law permits. We don't make the laws. We obey them."

Helping your employees or my students know "for sure" is something that we as leaders of our respective institutions ought to do more of. Values do matter—at school and at work—and their absence is a cancer at the very core of our community life.

My plea for business and education is that more than *doing* something we will *be* something, that individually and collectively we will cherish those personal values and individual standards that have marked the best of Western civilization for more than 2,000 years.

If it matters inside—inside the plant, inside the classroom, inside the office, inside the heart—then nothing on earth can keep it from mattering on the outside. May we believe in and foster such a shaping hand in our own destinies.

Elder Jeffrey R. Holland, now a member of the Council of the Twelve Apostles, The Church of Jesus Christ of Latter-day Saints, wrote this when he was president of Brigham Young University.

Chapter 51

Are Principles Enough?

By Thomas Riskas

*T*he paradoxes that face us all as leaders today are as numerous as are the "obvious" truths or principles that seem to guide our efforts. The problem we face is that the obvious principles we cling to are not the whole truth, and the whole truth is not obvious. Further, the naive employment of those obvious truths or principles that we are so sure of produce the very contradictions and inconsistencies that leave us in the grip of paradoxes we cannot understand and do not know how to deal with.

One such paradox involves our bias for action. The "bias for action" that characterizes our time is often redundant and one-sided as we seek to do what works within confined and inbred notions of effectiveness, appropriateness, or success. Meanwhile, our decisiveness and quick action can often cycle back in unexpected ways and set us back instead of moving us forward. The increased demands associated with management changes too often result in a frustrating tension between the need to push harder and the natural resistance that comes from being pushed.

Is it any wonder that most executives' concerns are pointed to decreased commitment and accountability and increased cynicism, frustration and insecurity. Programs, laws, policies, systems and strategies for order and improvement are often undermined by unconscious restraining forces that are more powerful than we can possibly imagine.

To resolve these tensions, leaders need to first understand and sense the difference between rationalization and reconciliation. To reconcile and transcend opposites to some higher truth does not involve rationalization or linear, logical thinking. It does, however, require systems thinking.

Leadership Tensions

Order	vs.	Chaos
Control	vs.	Release
Conformity	vs.	Dissent
Uniformity	vs.	Individuality
Long-term Growth and development	vs.	Short term profitability
Safety	vs.	Risk
Performance	vs.	Growth
Logic	vs.	Creativity
Profit	vs.	Social Responsibility
Follow the rules	vs.	Follow your judgement
Do what you're told	vs.	Do what is right
Direct	vs.	Support
Mission	vs.	Margin
Action	vs.	Inaction
Unilateral decision making	vs.	Consensus or Participative Decision making
The good of the many	vs.	The good of the few, or the one

Wisdom embraces a larger perspective for the highest good, and maturity considers others' interests in connection with our own. The ineffective or immature leader cannot hold the tension, but will quickly release one side in favor of the other to avoid delay and discomfort or the appearance of indecisiveness. The enlightened, more mature leader, conversely, sees the seed of each in the other and values both opposites in proper context. Thus, for example, from order springs chaos, which ushers in a higher order.

The issue is not either order or chaos but rather when should chaos be encourage and allowed in order to bring about a new order, and how should such chaos be managed to optimize the effect?

While principles and processes are important in dealing with such dilemmas, they are insufficient. The person's capacity to think systematically and hold the tension in ethically resolving competing demands and conflicting duties requires an entirely different kind of development that is essential to the leadership task, particularly in light of today's complex environment. Such development will necessarily focus on systems thinking, psychological wholeness, and managing the "hidden agenda" of the enterprise.

Deep within us is the center of our power and the source of lasting effectiveness. Here is where our abilities to love, influence, create and progress reside. Our center—our core—is the fountain of our integrity. Within it works our hidden agenda for wholeness and fulfillment.

Reaching the center is essential preparation for mature, wise leadership. Without doing so we can never achieve sustained effectiveness. Nor can we fully become the person that we are. To reach the center, we must peel off the layers of our own limitations.

These layers represent certain "levels of untruth" that act as barriers to our integrity and to the sustained effectiveness we seek. Overcoming these barriers requires that we face and convert our faulty beliefs to truth, humanize our inhuman expectations, heal the wounds that alienate us from ourselves and others, and expose the mechanisms we use so well to deceive ourselves and evade responsibility.

The Burden of Untruth

We have all learned the value of truth. Without truth there is no trust, no freedom, no growth, no joy. When we fail to face the truth and deal with it, we fail. The lies we live account for our tendencies to jump to conclusions, overreact, blame and accuse others, criticize and deceive ourselves, to name a few. They also turn our strengths to weaknesses. For example, consider the person whose "bias for action" becomes obsessive, impulsive and controlling, whose self-discipline becomes rigid, unyielding and insensitive, whose passion for excellence turns to intolerance and perfectionism, whose vast experience turns to dogmatism, or whose genuine care for others turns to dominance. These and countless other transformations have more to do with us than we might think. They are simply a psychological fact of life. As Joseph Campbell put it, "What's running the show is coming up from way down below."

Effectiveness Revisited

I believe we need to rethink the meaning of effectiveness and see the limitation in defining it simply in terms of self-discipline, performance, behavior or accomplishments, or in terms of how we spend our time, how much work we can do, how nice, sincere or competent we are, or how well we negotiate or get along with others. While these are certainly important aspects of effectiveness, they necessarily place a one-sided emphasis on human behavior and ignore the whole truth of the person. To quote C.S. Lewis:

> *There is an inextricable relationship between who we are, inside, and how we behave with others around us. But unless we begin first with the tidying up inside each human being, we are deceiving ourselves. What is the good of drawing up rules (ie. principles) of social behavior if we*

> *know in fact that our greed, cowardliness, ill temper, and self-conceit are going to prevent us from keeping them? I do not mean for a moment that we ought not to think and think hard about improvements in our social and economic system (or our organizations), but what I do mean is that all that thinking will be mere moonshine unless we realize that nothing but the courage and unselfishness of individuals is ever going to make any system work properly. Even when a system is changed, people who are twisted will find new ways to carry on the old game under the new system. You cannot make people good by law, and without good people you cannot have a good society.*

Perhaps being effective therefore, pertains more to a person's degree of consciousness, maturity, and wisdom than to some external standard or habitual form of behavior. While practicing effective behavior and adhering to principles can certainly be beneficial, it is no substitute for personal insight, depth perspective, and the care and integration of the soul. All are needed.

A New Developmental Agenda

I suggest that leaders in all walks of life learn to work beneath the surface, to achieve greater personal wholeness and sustained effectiveness. Such a developmental agenda might include:

1. *Understanding the layers of untruth that limit our effectiveness*, undermine our integrity, and frustrate our desire for wholeness and fulfillment. These layers include mechanisms of self-deceit, faulty beliefs, inhuman expectations and the false self.

2. *Learning how to* 1) *recognize* and rescript the false beliefs that alienate us from ourselves and others; 2) *align* our expectations with reality without compromising our standards; 3) *integrate* the inferior functions of our personality; 4) *defuse* our reactivity; and 5) *promote* greater self-honesty and personal healing.

3. *Learning how to attend to the needs of the soul.* Self-neglect kills the soul, disempowers the spirit, and makes us far less productive than we could be. By attending to our needs with empathy and imagination, we honor our reactivity and inconsistencies and learn to stop seeking perfection and to see with wisdom how our self-defeating behaviors are, in reality, the call of our soul to greater healing and wholeness.

Such an agenda demands expanded organizational responsibility and involvement in the personal and family domains. It requires us to work beneath the surface of behavioral and attitudinal prescriptions toward more complete self-knowledge, self-acceptance, and the ascent of wisdom, consciousness, and maturity.

And it requires us as leaders to create not only learning, principle-centered organizations, but healing organizations that are committed to personal empowerment through the "in depth" development of all its members. Such work, which enables us to get in relationship with ourselves, is fundamental to our success in living and working with others.

Thomas Riskas is the founder and president of Thomas Riskas & Associates, Inc, a consulting firm specializing in executive and in-tact team building, leadership development, and cultural transformation.

ABOUT THE EDITOR

Ken Shelton is chairman and editor-in-chief of *Executive Excellence* Publishing, publishers of newsletters, magazines, books, audio books, and CD-ROMs on personal and organizational development. The mission of *Executive Excellence* is to "help you find a wiser, better way to live your life and lead your organization."

Since 1984, Ken has served as editor of *Executive Excellence*, the world's leading executive advisory newsletter, and more recently *Personal Excellence*, a digest of the best thinking on personal and professional development. He is the editor of several books, including *In Search of Quality*, *A New Paradigm of Leadership*, and *The Best of Personal Excellence*.

For many years, he has enjoyed a close association with Stephen R. Covey, primarily as a writer and editor on various projects, including *The 7 Habits of Highly Effective People*, *Principle-Centered Leadership*, and *First Things First*. He is a former editor of *Utah Business* and *BYU Today* and a contributing writer to several other magazines.

Ken has a master's degree in mass and organizational communications from Brigham Young University and San Diego State University. In San Diego, California, he worked four years as a marketing communications specialist for General Dynamics Aerospace. He now lives in Provo, Utah, with his wife, Pam, and their three sons.

His book, *Beyond Counterfeit Leadership*, represents a creative synopsis of his writing and teaching, based on 30 years of professional experience, observation, and global travel.

Executive **Excellence**

Since 1984, *Executive Excellence* has provided business leaders and managers with the best and latest thinking on leadership development, managerial effectiveness, and organizational productivity. Each issue is filled with insights and answers from top business executives, trainers, and consultants—information you won't find in any other publication.

"Excellent! This is one of the finest newsletters I've seen in the field."

—Tom Peters, co-author of *In Search of Excellence*

"Executive Excellence *is the* Harvard Business Review *in* USA Today *format."*

—Stephen R. Covey, author of *The 7 Habits of Highly Effective People*

"Executive Excellence is the best executive advisory newsletter anywhere in the world—it's just a matter of time before a lot more people find that out."

—Ken Blanchard, co-author of *The One-Minute Manager*

CONTRIBUTING EDITORS INCLUDE

Stephen R. Covey

Ken Blanchard

Marjorie Blanchard

Charles Garfield

Peter Senge

Gifford Pinchot

Elizabeth Pinchot

Warren Bennis

Brian Tracy

Denis Waitley

For more information about *Executive Excellence* or *Personal Excellence*, or for information regarding books, audio tapes, CD-ROMs, custom editions, reprints, and other products, please call

Executive Excellence Publishing at:

1-800-304-9782

or visit our web site: **http://www.eep.com**

Personal Excellence

The Magazine of Life Enrichment

Our newest publication, *Personal Excellence*, is the magazine of life enrichment. As a value-based newsletter dedicated to personal and professional development, *Personal Excellence* focuses on such broad themes as Life-Career Balance, Spirit-Soul Enrichment, Health and Fitness, Relationships, Motivation, Mentoring, and Self-Esteem.

"I appreciate the quality and content . . ."

—John Naisbitt, author of *Megatrends* and *Megatrends 2000*

Contributing editors to *Personal Excellence* include:

Stephen R. Covey, author of *7 Habits of Highly Effective Families*
Ruth Stafford Peale, chairman of Guideposts, Inc.
Denis Waitley, author of *The Psychology of Winning*
Lou Tice, founder of the Winner's Circle Network
Dianna Booher, prolific author and motivational speaker
Ken Blanchard, co-author of *Everyone's a Coach*
Hyrum W. Smith, chairman of FranklinCovey Co.
Brian Tracy, author of *Maximum Achievement*

*"*Personal Excellence *is a very interesting and worthwhile publication that provides its readers with positive and beneficial reading material."*

—Tipper Gore, mental health policy advisor to President Clinton

Books of Related Interest from Executive Excellence Publishing

Executive Excellence
publications are perfect:

- *As personal or professional "vitamin pills."* Executive Excellence is an enriching monthly supplement to an executive's current diet of management and leadership training. *Personal Excellence* enhances the ongoing personal and professional development programs of people at any age and stage in life.

- *As in-house management or personal development newsletters.* The magazines can be customized and received under an organization's own cover sheet.

- *As thought pieces for focus groups and management meetings.* The magazines can be analyzed and applied to help with current organizational dilemmas.

- *As a public relations gesture.* The magazines can be sent to favored suppliers and customers or displayed in reception and reading areas.

- *As gifts.* Executive Excellence may be given to newly promoted managers or to a management segment of the company. *Personal Excellence* may be given to all employees as a benefit.

 ## Custom Corporate Editions
Corporate editions of both magazines are available. The magazine may be wrapped with a "false cover" with messages and announcements from the company, printed with the company logo, enhanced with articles by prominent company officers, or a combination.

 ## Custom Reprints
Order custom reprints of your favorite articles (or chapters in this book)—in black & white or color—for use in your corporate training and development programs and seminars.

 ## Foreign Language Editions
Executive Excellence is available in Korean, Japanese, and Turkish, editions. English-language editions for Australia, Ireland, and India are also available. *Personal Excellence* is available in Japanese and Turkish languages.

Executive Excellence Publishing has other publications in a variety of languages. For more information on other special editions, please call 1-800-304-9782.